No part of this book may be reproduced, or stored in a retrieval system, or transmitted in any form or by any means, electronic, mechanical, photocopying, recording, or otherwise, without express written permission of the publisher.

ISBN-13: 9798339255291

Cover design: Ann Carter
Front cover art: Matthew White
Back cover art: Jodie McConnell

Library of Congress Control Number: 2018675309
Printed in the United States of America

THE LAST GAME OF RUMMIKUB

Andrew Carter Curtis

Dedicated to my grandmother:
Hazel Camp Carter
December 12, 1917 – May 9, 2005

"Put God first in your life, and everything else will fall into place."

Table of Contents

Chapter 1: "So, when can you come back?"
Chapter 2: "The pitter patter of doggie feet"
Chapter 3: "This is my little sweetheart Jetta"
Chapter 4: "Celebrating the wisdom of age"
Chapter 5: "Elms"
Chapter 6: "Answer to my prayers"
Chapter 7: "The key is to be content during the hard times"
Chapter 8: "Thanksgiving"
Chapter 9: "The diagnosis"
Chapter 10: "What can make a relationship so strong"
Chapter 11: "Do y'all like to travel?"
Chapter 12: "And I always will"
Chapter 13: "Would have been good friends"
Chapter 14: "I know I never told y'all this"
Chapter 15: "The secret to parenting"
Chapter 16: "She too would fly again"
Chapter 17: "All those memories"
Chapter 18: "How much y'all have contributed to my life"
Chapter 19: "I want you two to have it"
Chapter 20: "May this game be a blessing"
Chapter 21: "Her name was Mrs. Jones"

Dear Mrs. Jones,

    Here is our written story, the one I told you about, the one I was working on a few years ago. You were so excited to read it, but I was not content with my first several drafts and therefore never sent it to you. You waited patiently, and now you are not here for me to share in the success of its completion. I realize through prayer that the book was never meant to be finished back then. I also know that you don't need to be here to read the story. Where you are now, you know the story I'm trying to tell better than the words on these pages. I plan to see you in that beautiful, flower-filled meadow we talked about. Thank you for all you have done for me and my family.

I love you,

Andrew

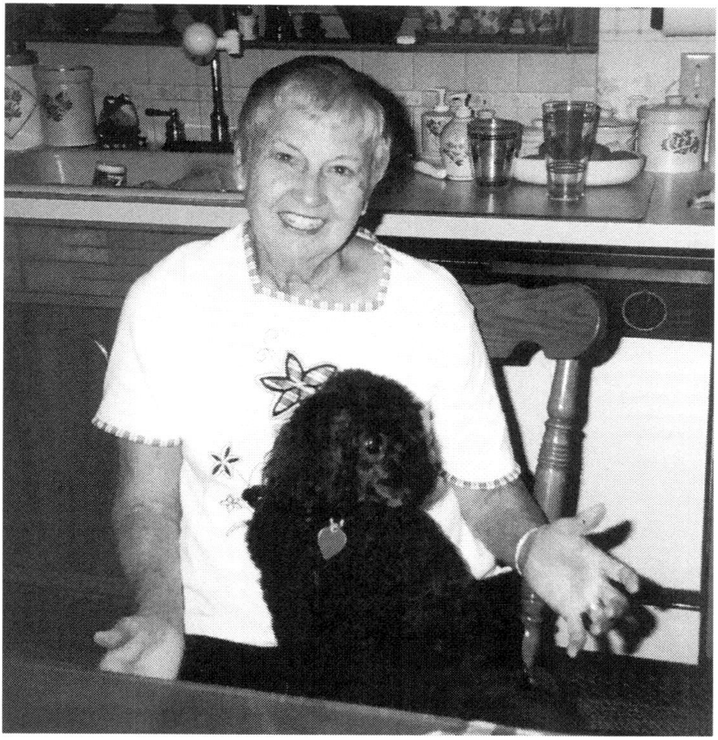

CHAPTER 1: "SO, WHEN CAN YOU COME BACK?"

"Did you see any interesting cases today, Andrew?" Mrs. Jones inquired with an intent look in her eyes.

My mind flashed back to the hectic workday I had just completed. "Actually, yes, as a matter of fact, I saw something that I have never seen before. A puppy ate an entire bottle of Gorilla Glue…"

…The poor dog looked miserable. His midsection was three times its normal size, and there was a disturbing groaning noise coming from within. Somehow this happy, eight-month-old labrador puppy was still wagging his tail. As I felt the rigid walls of the distended abdominal cavity, I listened to the owner describing how he had watched his dog chew and swallow a full bottle of Gorilla Glue. My mind was trying to piece together just how a small bottle could look like an inflated basketball in that animal's stomach. The radiograph images revealed a uniformly dense, round structure stretching the gastric walls to a ghastly diameter. Without question, this was a surgical case. Upon researching, I discovered that Gorilla Glue, when mixed with

stomach acid, would swell to a tremendous size. Now it made sense. The incision into the stomach was quite large, but I successfully extracted the enormous, firm foreign body and sutured the puppy closed. This little dog was going to be just fine...

"Well, who would have thought that Gorilla Glue could have caused such a problem?" Mrs. Jones said while staring down at her half-eaten dinner plate. "I would have figured that the glue could have been toxic, but never would I have dreamed that it would swell to the size you described."

"Me neither, Mrs. Jones, but nearly every day in this profession it seems that I see something I have never seen before."

"I always said I could have been a veterinarian as much as I love animals," Mrs. Jones said, almost regrettably, as she gazed down at her little black poodle, Jetta. As if sensing Mrs. Jones' longing, the sweet dog inched her way forward so that her owner could stroke her short, curly hair.

After supper, I assisted Mrs. Jones in cleaning the dishes and putting the leftover food away in Tupperware containers. I watched her hands work. So efficient. Surprisingly nimble. In utter defiance of her swollen joints, she toiled without complaint. Rather, she sang softly, an old

Baptist hymn that I did not recognize at first. She sang as if she had no cares in the world.

"I have always said that no matter how blue you are, no matter how bad things are going for you, you can always sing. Singing is a way of praising God," she spoke while peering out the window above the sink, overlooking her garage. "My old voice doesn't sound like it once did. I used to sing in the church and loved it. God gave me a strong voice, so I sang."

"I'm not sure too many people would like the sound of my singing, Mrs. Jones!" I joked.

"It doesn't matter. Sing for yourself. It has a way of opening up the soul." She spoke seriously as she dried the last dish.

"Let's go in the den and sit down, Andrew. Right this way."

I followed patiently behind Mrs. Jones shuffling over the linoleum floor to the dark blue carpet of the den. She plopped down with a sigh on one of the two couches, so I sat on the other.

To my left was a large bay window with a cushioned seat overlooking the backyard. Many shelves clung to the walls all the way up to the ceiling and were adorned with an assortment of knick-knacks and collectables. On the very top, ringing the room, was the apparently entire collection of stuffed animal Beanie Babies in mint condition with the tags still dangling from each ear.

No sooner than we took our seats on the couch, Jetta launched her tiny frame up onto Mrs. Jones' lap and looked at me with an open-mouth grin.

Mrs. Jones noticed my gazing at the shelves around the room and spoke with a laugh, "Yes, I like to collect things."

Everything seemed to be neatly arranged with the space utilized efficiently. Surprisingly, the house did not have a cluttered feel but rather a warm, comforting aura of home. I could appreciate her spirit of interest in a variety of items.

Seeing her well-manicured yard as I stared out the bay window to my left, I remarked admiringly, "Mrs. Jones, I love your yard. You sure seem to have a green thumb."

"I love gardening, Andrew. It gets harder and harder for me to get outside though. My joints just won't allow it much anymore. I have a wonderful landscaper who comes weekly to tend to my flower beds. Did you notice my pretty cosmos still in bloom out front?"

"I wasn't sure what kind of flowers those were," I admitted, remembering the vibrant, orange petals. "But they do look great where you planted them."

She shifted slightly to face me better. "Actually, Andrew, I just scatter the seeds every year and they come up like that. No planting necessary. Just throw them out."

She rolled her "R" as she spoke the word "throw," and I laughed to myself. I did not know at the time that this is how she would always speak the word, with a roll of her tongue.

"They are my favorite flowers. They come in all colors, but I am partial to the orange ones," she said gazing out the window.

As I thought about the flowers in her front yard, I remembered the lush tree by her driveway that I had seen as I arrived. The small, plentiful leaves were beginning to show a pale yellow of fall.

"Mrs. Jones, what kind of tree is that right by your driveway?"

"It's an elm," she responded excitedly. "Isn't it beautiful? I planted it right there, shaped it, and have watched it grow. Elms are fast growing and make excellent shade trees."

"That would be a good tree to plant in my yard," I said, imagining the direct afternoon sun. "I could use a shade tree or two on the west side of my yard."

"Every spring I have a few volunteer baby elms sprouting up. I want you to get some. You can take as many as you would like," she offered while making a sweeping motion with her thin arm. "The elm tree has always been my favorite tree. So beautiful. So dense. So hearty. And the autumn yellow... well, you will just have to see it in a few more weeks."

I could already picture where I wanted to plant a couple. I smiled, "Yes ma'am, I would like to have some from you."

She continued staring out the window as the daylight slowly faded. "Next time you visit we will have to take a walk in my yard before we eat supper. My yard-man does a super job of maintaining my flowers. Ever since Leonard died, I have needed an extra hand around here."

Mrs. Jones transferred her gaze to a cluster of framed pictures on one of the side tables across from the couch. "See that picture right there?" She pointed a frail finger, cruelly curved by her ruthless joint disease. "That's Leonard when he was in the Navy. Leonard was my second husband. And that picture there... Yes, that was Cecil, my first husband. He also served in the Navy. After he passed away, I married Leonard."

Mrs. Jones paused and stared at the black TV screen as if watching her memories dance to life.

"I married Cecil a long time ago. We were both raised in Tallahassee, and that's where we stayed our entire married life. I spent many years working for FSU (Florida State University) until I retired in '93."

"What did you do at FSU?" I asked.

She looked up and smiled. "I was in charge of graduate admissions. Had 144 grad students at one time. Some of the faculty did not care about these students, but I did. I tried to look after them, you know, help them the best that I could. I'm glad I got the chance to help so many outstanding people in my lifetime."

Mrs. Jones cleared her throat and shifted on the couch cushion. "Cecil was like that too. Loved helping others. He was a wonderful man. My first love. We had a beautiful life there in Tallahassee, but he passed away nearly twenty years ago, in '95. Oh, I wish he were here for you to meet now. You would have loved him."

"I would have loved to meet him, too," I responded.

"After Cecil died, I married Leonard. That was in '98. See, I had known Leonard all my life. He told me that he had actually always loved me but never had the courage to ask me on a date way back when. It's funny how things work out like that. God put us together at last. I had told myself that I didn't need to remarry because I loved Cecil so much and created an amazing life with him.

It came as a mighty big shock when Leonard approached the topic of marrying me. I had to give it some thought, but then I realized how kind of a man he was." She laughed and continued, "Now I can say that I am truly blessed to have had two exceptionally great husbands in my life."

I grinned: "Yes, I guess not too many women can say that!"

Looking at the pictures, I imagined her former life in Tallahassee.

"What brought you to Tifton, Georgia then?" I asked curiously.

"Leonard was from the Tifton area and had retired from the Navy, and since my mother and kin were from around here, Osierfield to be exact, we decided to buy this house and move here. A new start, you could say. I knew plenty of people in this town already, and it's not too far from Tallahassee."

Staring at the pictures on the table in front of us, I noticed a couple of children also pictured. My curiosity wanted to inquire about these children, but I decided not to pry.

Here was a lady in her 80s, living with no one other than her dog and battling an array of medical problems-- a sudden loneliness pushed down on me until I looked back up at Mrs. Jones. She was smiling, obviously still reminiscing about her life. No self-pity there.

I noticed a small, framed, black and white picture of a young woman who closely resembled Mrs. Jones and asked, "Is that your mom?"

"It sure is. Everyone says that I look so much like her." She paused for a few seconds. "I wish I had known her. She died when I was three. She was 33. The doctor back then said she died of tuberculosis, but my uncle never believed it. He was convinced she died from something else... like cancer." She cleared her throat before continuing. "I get my love of music from her. My dad said she could sing, play the piano, and even taught violin lessons."

"Do you play any instruments, Mrs. Jones?"

Her smile softened: "I used to play the piano. Matter of fact, I taught myself how to play. These old, crooked fingers won't let me play anymore. Oh, how I would love to play again though. There is nothing quite like the soothing sound of piano strings."

I lost track of time as we continued to talk, but the jarring buzz of the pager on my belt brought me back to reality. Then the deep, echoing chime of a grandfather clock from another room boomed out nine resounding notes. I knew without even returning the emergency call that I would have to leave. I just had a feeling; my pager had been too quiet for too long.

"Duty calls," I said, pointing to the pager.

I reluctantly rose off the couch and offered my hand to assist Mrs. Jones.

"Thank you, dear," she said with a strained sigh while struggling to her feet.

As I slowly weaved my way around the couch and tables, I noticed a black cowboy hat hanging to the right of the kitchen door next to a picture of Leonard and Mrs. Jones posing together within a gold, oval frame. Both were so happy.

Mrs. Jones reached up delicately to hug my neck, and over her bony shoulder I looked into Leonard's friendly eyes. He appeared to be a kind man, one of the many reminders of the good in Mrs. Jones's life.

"Oh, you almost forgot your leftover food!" Mrs. Jones excitedly remembered.

Grabbing two plastic containers from the refrigerator, she said, "Next time I hope your darling wife can join us. I would love to meet her. So, when can you come back?"

I thought for a moment. "How about next Tuesday? I'm on call again next Tuesday."

The delight in her eyes radiated her happy mood. "Tuesday it is! But you are welcome anytime. You can drop by unannounced if you want to. I just want to see your smiling face again."

Taking the food containers from her, I hugged Mrs. Jones again, knelt down to pat a wiggly Jetta on her head, and stepped outside into the cooling October air. I exited the open garage door and glanced back at the sign to the left of the breezeway door: NO HOME IS COMPLETE WITHOUT THE PITTER PATTER OF DOGGIE FEET.

Once at my truck, I peered up at the shadowy elm tree in the dim light emitted from the house. I knew I would be returning to see Mrs. Jones and Jetta again. After one visit, it already felt like home.

CHAPTER 2: "THE PITTER PATTER OF DOGGIE FEET"

Mrs. Jones's favorite elm tree awaited our arrival the next Tuesday as Leigh and I pulled into the driveway.

Exiting my truck, I softly touched the elm's bark, feeling its unique texture beneath my fingers. Smooth yet flaky-- similar to a crape myrtle.

The garage door, like the previous visit, was closed but suddenly lurched to life. Mrs. Jones must have been watching through the window, eager to welcome her company. Into the neatly organized garage we walked, past Mrs. Jones's silver Chevy Impala, and to the breezeway door. I looked to the left of the door and read the sign aloud to Leigh.

"No home is complete without the pitter patter of doggie feet," I smiled just imagining Mrs. Jones and her happy little dog inside.

We walked through the door leading into the breezeway and then up the three brick steps. The scratching of claws on the linoleum floor and the jingle of Jetta's collar could be heard on the other side of the kitchen door. Before we could knock, Mrs. Jones pulled open the door with a radiant smile stretched across her face.

"Hey, Y'all!" Mrs. Jones shouted, tossing her hands above her head. "Andrew, you didn't tell me she was so beautiful!" she exclaimed, reaching for Leigh's neck to hug.

Leigh blushed at the doting attention and gave Mrs. Jones a hug. Stepping inside behind Leigh, I quietly shut the door and gave Mrs. Jones a soft hug too. Jetta danced in happy circles around our feet, and we bent over to pat the little greeter on her head.

"Sit down. Sit down," Mrs. Jones excitedly commanded with a dramatic sweep of her hands, pointing to the dining table chairs. "Supper is almost ready, and I want you two to relax."

"No, ma'am," Leigh and I said in unison. "We want to help you."

Mrs. Jones did not resist our offer.

Assisting in setting the table and finishing the cooking, we chatted with Mrs. Jones, primarily about Leigh's entertaining medical stories at the hospital, which Mrs. Jones listened to with focused anticipation.

"So, you work in the ICU?" Mrs. Jones asked Leigh.

"Yes ma'am. I'm with Pulmonology and Critical Care, but I don't do any office visits. I just work twelve hour shifts at the hospital."

"I guess you see some really sick people in there." Mrs. Jones paused for a few seconds, rubbing her ear. "It takes a special person to do what you do. I can see how caring you are. You are doing what God wants you to do."

I smiled to myself. Mrs. Jones had a way of making a person feel a sense of purpose.

We ladled the steaming vegetable soup into our bowls and set them on the dinner table. Mrs. Jones wrapped the hot bread rolls into a small, white hand towel and placed them in a wicker basket. Next, I waited for Mrs. Jones to sit so I could scoot her closer to the table.

"Thank you, honey," Mrs. Jones said, barely above a whisper.

I walked around the table to sit across from her, and Leigh sat beside me.

"Andrew, would you say the blessing please?" Mrs. Jones asked, already closing her eyes and bowing her head.

My blessing was concluded with a statement from Mrs. Jones. "And thank you, Lord, for bringing this sweet, young couple into my life."

Opening my eyes, I dipped my spoon into the soup and looked across at Mrs. Jones.

"So, Andrew, any interesting vet cases today?" Mrs. Jones asked.

I peeked down at little Jetta who was staring patiently up at me with a curious look on her face, as if she, too, was awaiting my response.

"Yes ma'am. I had a very interesting situation today…"

…The dog's owners were adamant. Their one-year-old husky mix DID NOT get into anything. This was in response to one of my often used questions to pet owners whenever their pets were not well: Could the pet have ingested anything toxic? This patient today was unable to stand and appeared to be worsening by the minute. My mind kept returning to a potential toxic cause, but the owners stuck to their original story that their dog never went out of their sight. The only change in their routine was the day before to go for a walk with their dog on a trail in the woods. But the dog DID NOT go out of their sight! After my initial exam, bloodwork, and radiographs revealed no clues, I decided to start IV fluids while I ruminated on the strange occurrence. Frustration mounted as I saw my patient now laterally recumbent on my treatment table. What could be causing this apparent body paralysis to such a healthy, young dog without any further symptoms? Desperately, I searched the dog again as I felt a sinking feeling of dread in fighting a losing battle. Then, there it was! Could it really be? It only looked like a speck in the dog's ear, but as I leaned in closer, the details of

the tiny parasite became apparent. Tick paralysis! A strange phenomenon can occur rarely when a tick's saliva emits a potent, paralyzing neurotoxin that can take down even a large breed dog. However, the grave-sounding condition is easily rectified by simply removing the tick. That's all. Within hours, an immobile body can return to normal function. And so it was with this young husky. By the end of the workday, the pet and its owners were reunited in a joyous embrace of celebrated recovery. How I wish all my cases turned out this well...

Mrs. Jones looked past me, staring at the opposite wall for a few seconds, digesting the almost unbelievable recovery tale. "Hmm. I never knew a tick could paralyze a dog like that. It must be rewarding to be able to help these critters," she said while stretching a bony, crooked finger towards Jetta's nose. The happy dog licked her owner's blotched hand. "You have a gift, Andrew."

"I don't always feel like I have a gift," I laughed as I thought of the difficulties of my job. "They don't all live happily ever after."

"You must keep faith and know that you are doing the best you can do. I know you can't heal every animal that comes to you, but please don't lose sight of all the good you do." Mrs. Jones spoke convincingly. "That's why they call it 'practicing medicine,' right?"

The three of us laughed.

"Yes ma'am. I suppose you are right about that." I took another bite of the tasty soup.

Studying Mrs. Jones in front of me, I thought of my grandmother, Mama Hazel. Those encouraging words could have just as well come from Mama Hazel. I felt a strange connection to my youth and relished the moment.

After supper, the three of us cleared the table of plates and silverware and cleaned the dishes. As Mrs. Jones scrubbed, she burst into an upbeat song, the lyrics flowing from her bright spirit.

Turning to us with a beaming smile, Mrs. Jones asked, "Have y'all ever played Rummikub?" There was a sparkle in her eyes.

"No ma'am. I have never even heard of it," I admitted. Neither had Leigh.

"Oh wonderful! Just wonderful! I will teach you. Andrew, will you look under the sofa? There is a basket under there with the game case in it."

Obediently, I walked the few paces to the couch and peeked underneath. Jetta, who had followed me, promptly licked my face repeatedly, darting side to side as I turned my head, laughing. Grasping the worn wicker basket, I carried it to the kitchen table. Mrs. Jones gleamed as she flipped up the two metal buckles holding the red, green, and brown leather case shut. As she lifted the top, I peered inside.

"I absolutely love this game. It's my favorite," she exclaimed, fingering one of the game pieces. "I know y'all will love it too. Here, let me show you."

Dumping the contents of the case in a haphazard mound, Mrs. Jones began to rummage through the numbered game tiles. Each tile was assigned a number, one through thirteen, and was colored either black, blue, red, or green. After drawing fourteen random tiles, the objective was to be the first to eliminate all the tiles in one's possession by forming them into sets of runs and groups. Excitedly, Mrs. Jones explained the details of the game and offered basic strategy suggestions. Much like a card game, we chatted idly while wearing poker faces as we plotted our next moves. Mrs. Jones did not disguise her competitive spirit and easily won the first couple of rounds. Occasionally, she would hum a tune while planning her next move. A smile remained on her face.

The time was nearly 10 PM when we stood to leave. Leigh and I both had to work the following day and had a 30-minute drive home. But we were to learn that we could never leave Mrs. Jones quickly, the Southern hostess that she was.

The grandfather clock in the adjacent room struck out ten deep notes that echoed through the house. No stopping time, it reminded me.

Mrs. Jones packed some leftover soup for us to take home, and Jetta pranced around our legs. I knelt to the floor to pet Jetta on the head. What a great, little dog for a special lady--both needed each other.

Throwing her arms above her head, Mrs. Jones squeezed my neck tightly and kissed me on the cheek.

"Y'all come back now."

I smiled and assured her we would.

I glanced to my left at the silent, black cowboy hat hanging on the wall next to Leonard's picture, a reminder of what was gone in Mrs. Jones's life. But before the sorrow could creep in, I looked back at the elderly lady and her dog. So happy.

No home is complete without the pitter patter of doggie feet.

CHAPTER 3: "THIS IS MY LITTLE SWEETHEART, JETTA"

Several months prior, I had been working a typical day at the veterinary clinic, hustling to keep up with the ever-increasing demands of the profession. In a sense, I felt caught in a rut. Day in, day out, working harder than I ever had just to try to keep up.

Robotically, I snatched the next awaiting medical chart from the walk-in slot and briskly made my way down the hall to one of the exam rooms. Opening the door, I peeked inside.

I saw a woman sitting on the red built-in bench seat holding a small, black poodle. Instantly, something felt different, different in a calming sense. There was a connection before I even entered the room.

My mind rapidly processed the scene before me: the woman's neatly clipped, short, gray hair, her enlarged, bony knees and knuckles, her splotchy, dry skin. She wore long, dark green shorts with a white blouse and white shoes. A genuine smile spread across her face showing two rows of well-aligned, bright teeth below a pair of trusting, light brown eyes. There was a familiarity that I hadn't yet acknowledged.

Offering my hand in greeting, I said, "I'm Andrew Curtis. Nice to meet you."

Extending her trembling hand, she said, "I'm Frances Jones, and this is my little sweetheart, Jetta."

She had one hand on Jetta's back while the little dog danced happily in her owner's lap. The miniature poodle seemed a proper fit for the elderly lady before me. I gazed admiringly at Jetta and looked into her spirited little eyes. I knew immediately. This was a dog I could trust. Those eyes radiated kindness and warmth.

No, she would not bite, I knew. Far too many dogs "won't bite," but oh, beware the dog that "won't bite!" More than one pet owner has confidently reported to me that their dogs would never bite a soul, only to find out that their judgement of canine temperament had been amiss.

Yes indeed. This was truly a sweet dog looking back at me.

"What's going on with Jetta today?" I asked as I thumbed through the brief medical record.

"She just keeps pawing at this ear of hers and shaking her head. I am worried that she might have an ear infection," Mrs. Jones sighed, massaging one of Jetta's ears.

Gently scooping the little dog into my arms, I placed her on the exam table in the center of the small, private room of the animal hospital. No need for an otoscope to yield the diagnosis. I curiously leaned over to peer into Jetta's right ear and observed the undeniable redness and dark wax accumulation that accompanies a canine ear infection. Out of habit, I inserted my nose mere inches from the unsightly aural opening only to revolt at the putrid odor. Veterinarians are comically magnetized to the horrid sensory stimulations that our health profession has to offer, but we are trained in such a way. We need all the clues that we can get to aid in a diagnosis.

Lightly lifting the other ear flap, I searched thoroughly for any signs that it, too, might be problematic, but as is sometimes the case, only one ear proved affected.

"Yes ma'am, you are correct. Your little Jetta does have a pretty significant ear infection here," I reported while lifting the right ear flap. "I'm going to need to clean this outer rim area, and then we will send some medicated drops for you to administer at home. Do you think you will have a difficult time applying the drops?"

"No, not at all," Mrs. Jones smiled convincingly at me, then at her dog.

Standing so obediently on the exam table,

Jetta suddenly looked familiar.

"Do you use a groomer here?" I inquired.

"Yes, I have been using Carrie for a while now. She does a wonderful job. I used to groom all my dogs through the years, but my joints just won't allow it anymore."

An imaginary twinge of pain shot through my body as I studied Mrs. Jones's swollen joints.

At that moment, I witnessed another familiarity before me. Mrs. Jones reminded me of my own grandmother, Mama Hazel, my mother's mom. Her smile. Her eyes. The way she spoke. Even her mannerisms. Mama Hazel had passed away nearly a decade before but remained in my life through treasured memories.

My job as a veterinarian afforded me a plethora of relationship opportunities, but this meeting felt different somehow. Something special was quickly developing between us that I could not quite decipher at the time. But I felt it.

I have always experienced an emotion of deep respect for the elderly. My being 28 years old at the time, I believe I subconsciously sought the wisdom from someone over half a century older than I.

Exiting the room briefly, I returned clutching a small blue and white bottle of medicated ear ointment.

"This is a fairly new ear medication," I explained while holding the label close to Mrs. Jones for her to see. "It works really well, and it's cheaper than the others we have."

Mrs. Jones smiled and straightened her back as she spoke, "You may want to say, 'less expensive' rather than 'cheaper. Cheaper' implies poor quality to me."

I could not suppress the grin that overtook my expressions. Definitely a comment that Mama Hazel would have made. I understood completely.

"Good point... it's less expensive than the others," I lightheartedly rephrased.

Twisting off the top of the small bottle, I leaned over to dispense some of the viscous liquid into the affected ear while Jetta stood calmly. Oh, how I wish all patients were as well behaved as she!

"You see, I put about that much of the medicine in the ear and then gently massage the base of the ear canal. Only needs to be done once daily."

"Oh yes, Miss Priss will stand perfectly still for me at home," Mrs. Jones proudly reported with a beaming smile stretched across her line-laden face.

"Ok then. Let's plan to see y'all back in two weeks for a recheck."

Carefully handing Jetta back to Mrs. Jones,

I did not fully appreciate the importance of this encounter.

Clipping the leash to Jetta's pink collar, Mrs. Jones peered up at me with a gracious expression and said, "We will see you in a couple of weeks. Thank you for seeing Jetta today."

She set Jetta on the floor at her feet and rocked herself to gain momentum to rise. Mrs. Jones's wobbly legs braced her to an upright position as I stood ready to catch her should she fall. I nodded my head with a smile, opened the door to the exam room, and watched as Jetta happily led Mrs. Jones slowly out into the lobby.

On to another patient I went, but there would be no forgetting Mrs. Jones and Jetta.

CHAPTER 4: "CELEBRATING THE WISDOM OF AGE"

In South Georgia, the fall comes late, and the spring comes early. At last, the first true cold days of the season came on this overcast, mid-November day. I steered my truck into the now familiar driveway at 604 East 12th Street to park under Mrs. Jones's favorite elm tree. No green was to be seen today on its branches. All leaves had turned to a bright yellow, a kind of yellow that looks alive even in the absence of direct sunlight. This tree had morphed into a welcomed picture of autumn, just like Mrs. Jones had said it would.

My upward gazing was interrupted by the noisy clanging of the garage door beginning to open. Peeling my stare away from the yellow foliage above, I entered the garage. The sign to the left of the breezeway door would soon be brought to life, I knew; I now anticipated the soft "pitter patter of doggie feet" and tapping of dog nails on the other side of the wall. Through the breezeway, up the few brick steps, and to the kitchen door I went. I stood and waited until I heard the muffled rustling on the other side. The door opened before I could knock.

"Hey, Andrew! Come in. Come in." Mrs. Jones commanded with a dramatic wave of her hands.

The house smelled of freshly cooked food as I stepped inside. Jetta was craving my greeting, standing on her hind legs and whining softly.

"Hey, Mrs. Jones! Thanks for having me over again," I said. "Leigh will be here shortly. She is just now getting off work."

I hugged Mrs. Jones's frail body, and she kissed me on the cheek. I smelled the distinct perfume on her clothes and the aroma of a home-cooked meal blending warmly. This was already a place I loved, eliciting memories of spending time long ago with my grandparents.

"You better say hey to Miss Priss Tail down there. I do believe she looks forward to your visits as much as I do!" Mrs. Jones laughed, pointing a thin finger toward Jetta.

"Well, hey to you too, Jetta," I said as I scratched her head.

Like always, once Jetta considered that I had given her a proper greeting, she pranced to her spot on the linoleum floor between the stove and dining table and plopped down with a look of contentment.

I followed Mrs. Jones the short distance to the stove where she had prepared baked chicken quarters, corn on the cob, green bean casserole, and bread rolls.

Handing me the serving tongs, Mrs. Jones said, "Here, you fix your plate first."

I shook my head. "No ma'am. You first," I said respectfully. "Thank you for the offer, but please get yours first."

The stubborn look on her face made me laugh, so I began filling my plate. There was always more than enough food for our meals because Mrs. Jones intended to send us home with leftovers.

Sitting at the table, Mrs. Jones and I talked while we waited for Leigh to arrive.

"Any interesting vet cases today, Andrew?" Mrs. Jones asked with a wink of her eye.

"Of course! There is always something unusual in my workday," I laughed. "Well, let's see. There was a cat that gave me a fit this morning..."

...Just a neuter. Shouldn't take long. These were the surgeries I liked to see when I was running behind schedule. The morning, like usual, had started out a bit hectic. With an emergency case thrown into the mix, I was fighting the clock to make my rounds. Now I was preparing to neuter a tom cat quickly and then jump back into some appointments. The procedure went routinely, but the recovery was atypical, with an alarmingly bloody incision site. I did tie off the blood vessels correctly, right? I double

checked to be sure. Yes, the spermatic cord with its arterial supply was tied tightly with no leakage, but the skin incision was oozing quite persistently, long after it should have clotted. Why was this feline not clotting? His bloodwork panel was within normal limits. His mucous membranes were still pink so no significant blood loss yet. I pondered the situation. What would cause delayed blood clotting? Rat poison? We veterinarians are trained to throw this seemingly ubiquitous toxin into the rule-out list whenever an unexplainable bleeding event occurs. Calling the owner immediately, I discovered that this cat had vomited "something green" hours before, and when inquired about the use of rat poison, the owner nonchalantly said that, yes, he did indeed have rat bait out (which was green) but that it was tucked safely behind the freezer where "a cat can't get to it." Oh, but the cat did get to it. Fortunately, this particular type of poison has an antidote— vitamin K— if the condition is diagnosed early enough. After injecting the cat with the life-saving treatment, I prepared a prescription of vitamin K for a few weeks to send home with the owner, but first, this patient would need close monitoring at the vet hospital. He would, in fact, be ok after all...

Mrs. Jones was smiling at me and reached for my arm. "I absolutely love the stories that turn out well. That's a lucky cat to have you doctor him."

I sighed and glanced down. "Wish all my cases recovered like that."

"Well, you just have to look at the positive ones and believe in yourself," she said optimistically.

A knock at the door interrupted our chat.

"Oh, look who it is. Must be Leigh!" Despite her arthritis, Mrs. Jones shuffled to the door with surprising speed and turned the lock.

Stepping inside, my wife hugged Mrs. Jones.

"Come on in, honey. We just served our plates and were waiting on you before we started to eat." Mrs. Jones spoke excitedly.

"I hope y'all haven't been waiting too long," Leigh apologized.

"We haven't, Leigh. And I hope you did not rush to get here. I know your job at the hospital is demanding. Here, right this way. Come serve your plate, and do get all you want. I made plenty for y'all." Mrs. Jones handed Leigh a plate and the serving tongs.

While fixing her plate, Leigh asked, "Have you been feeling alright, Mrs. Jones?"

The reply came quickly: "Yes, yes, I'm doing fine. Don't worry about me."

Mrs. Jones routinely deflected questions about her ailments and would often simply change the subject.

"I hear you just had a birthday, Leigh. Tell me, did you have a good day? I hope you were pampered!" Mrs. Jones laughed.

Leigh looked over her shoulder from her position at the stove. "Yes ma'am. I did have a fun birthday. Speaking of birthdays, when is your birthday, Mrs. Jones?"

"Next month, actually. December 30th. I will be 83." She showed a proud, resilient smile.

I was surprised at her vitality and calculated the math in my head. "So, you were born in 1930?" I asked in admiration of her generation.

"Sure was. Right in the midst of the Great Depression," she said. "We learned a lot in those days. We didn't have much materially, but we had our families. Truth is, no one had much, but we didn't know any better. We were so happy. I'm afraid kids nowadays are losing sight of what's really important in life. And respect for the elderly... it's not like it used to be. We should all be learning from the lessons of older people. We should be celebrating the wisdom of age and experience."

I pondered the last sentence she spoke. Perhaps that simple statement summed up one of my longings for friendships with elderly folks. I was seeking this wisdom of age and did not even fully realize it.

As Leigh sat down in her chair at the old dining table, Mrs. Jones asked, "Andrew, will you please say the blessing?"

"Sure, Mrs. Jones," I responded while bowing my head.

After the blessing, Mrs. Jones looked at Leigh and said, "Tell us about your day, dear."

Leigh forced a weak smile. "It was ok," she said. "We really got busy after lunch, but it is a full moon, so we expected some craziness. We have a joke about working in the medical field on a full moon."

"I agree!" I offered my opinion. I certainly understood the wacky phenomenon of a full moon's influence on medical cases.

Mrs. Jones shook her head. "I have never heard that before. There are many things in this world that we can't explain. But I believe God has a hand in it all."

After cleaning the dishes and putting away the leftover food, Mrs. Jones directed me to retrieve the basket under the couch which held her leather Rummikub case. This game had become our sure routine. Even Jetta knew what to do as she followed me to the sofa. When I leaned down to grasp the wicker basket, Jetta excitedly licked me over and over on the nose, and I could hear Mrs.

Jones and Leigh laughing at my situation.

We talked as we always would, half distracted by the mind's competitive involvement in the game, and time seemed to slip away from the room. This plain dining table held a certain spell of being able to evaporate the world of time we were in, allowing me to disconnect from the stressors of the day.

"Oops, Andrew, look what you missed. You could have put your blue 4 and 5 right there and continued a good run," Mrs. Jones said with a crafty grin. "Looks like I will have to take advantage of that spot!" She laughed heartily at my error. I laughed too, reveling in the fact that this nearly 83 year old lady had a mind sharper than mine. Kindly, she would often point out my missed opportunities in the game, coaching me as we played. Though competitive, Mrs. Jones never chose "winning" over "teaching" me how to improve.

"I'm slowly catching on, Mrs. Jones," I joked. "Just be patient with me. One of these days I will win a round!"

At one point, I glanced down at our feet and looked at Jetta lying so peacefully. Her eyes were half shut with a sleepy, peaceful look on her face. I gazed around the room at all of Mrs. Jones's belongings and thought how fortunate I was to be a part of her life.

With the old grandfather clock's reminding, we finished the game and rose from our chairs. Hugging Mrs. Jones in the doorway of her home, I glanced at Leonard's black hat on the wall, like I always would. I also scanned the room at the many Beanie Babies high on the wall peering down at us and thought optimistically of the wonderful times ahead.

"Oh, y'all please come back soon. I just love having you two over. You are one of the sweetest couples I have ever met," Mrs. Jones stated proudly.

The little dog at my feet pranced around until she got my attention.

"Bye bye, Jetta." I knelt down and saw an almost human attraction deep in those dark eyes. "Mrs. Jones, you sure do have a special dog here." I stood to leave, and Mrs. Jones hugged my neck again.

"You will never know how much I appreciate your caring for Jetta. She means the world to me. Not sure what I would do without her."

Studying the happy pair, I realized that I did not wish to imagine their being apart.

CHAPTER 5: "ELMS"

"Hey, Andrew, come in! Come in!" Mrs. Jones said with a light in her eyes. She reached up and swung her frail arms around my neck. I felt her kiss on my cheek and smelled her perfume, mixed with the kitchen's aroma.

"Hey, Mrs. Jones. How have you been?" I asked, bending over to pat Jetta who was happily dancing in place at my feet with her claws tapping quietly on the linoleum.

"I'm hanging in there, you know. But how have you been?" Again, she chose to evade her own problems.

"I have been doing well," I responded. "I'm happy to report that I see some signs of spring out there," I said pointing in the direction of the front yard. "That redbud tree right outside looks welcoming with its little purple blooms."

Mrs. Jones's smile widened. "Oh, don't you just love a redbud? What about the daffodils? Did you notice mine? They just opened this week, too. We know that spring is right around the corner," she sang, clapping her hands together. Mrs. Jones spoke of spring with a fervor that comes from one who loves nature.

A car door slammed shut outside, and Mrs. Jones exclaimed excitedly, "Must be Leigh!"

Moments later, we could hear the breezeway door open and shut, but before Leigh could knock on the kitchen door, Mrs. Jones swung it open to greet Leigh with a welcoming hug.

"And how is my favorite Physician's Assistant doing today?" Mrs. Jones asked, beaming a huge smile.

"I'm doing great, Mrs. Jones, especially now that I'm here. How have you been doing?" Leigh asked.

"I'm making it... but don't you worry about me. Come in and eat. I'm sure you are starving." Mrs. Jones waved her hand to the direction of the stove where the hot food awaited.

On Mrs. Jones's command, we prepared our plates of chicken and rice, sweet potatoes, white acre peas, and corn bread muffins.

"Andrew, will you please say the blessing?" Mrs. Jones asked, already closing her eyes in prayer and clasping her hands together.

"Of course, Mrs. Jones."

We all bowed our heads as I thanked God.

Then came the question that Mrs. Jones loved to ask me.

"Any interesting vet cases today, Andrew?"

"Yes ma'am. I'm a bit embarrassed to admit

this one because I almost missed something I shouldn't have…"

…Sometimes we can just tell. There wasn't much need for a lengthy exam to know that this dog was dying. As I entered the exam room, the 12-year-old Boykin spaniel was in a state of shock with labored breaths. I quickly listened to its chest with my stethoscope and could not hear anything but extremely muffled heart and lung sounds. The owner explained that the symptoms started the day prior but had progressively gotten worse. Given the dog's age, cancer was high on my list of potential causes, despite the seemingly acute onset of signs. Many times, an animal's body can compensate remarkably well as cancer takes its hold, and then suddenly, the body can do no more to combat the issue. The symptoms can arise suddenly even though the underlying disease may be chronic. Chest radiographs revealed what I already suspected— a horribly affected thoracic cavity, with very little recognition of basic structures. I hung my head as I thought how to word the heartbreaking diagnosis to the worried owner. Stepping away from the X-ray screen, I meandered through the hallway to view my patient again, who was now on our treatment table away from the owner in the examination room. Yes, this was terminal. Surely it was. He looked bad… really bad. At times like this, watching a pet fighting for

breath in an agonizing strain, literally suffocating, I feel that euthanasia is a medical blessing. I took a deep breath, scooped the Boykin into my arms, and made my way back to the anxiously awaiting owner. Something in my mind told me to glance at the radiographs one more time. As I passed the monitor screen, I stopped in my tracks. Did I really miss the diagnosis? My eyes were immediately "opened." The obvious gas pockets indicating loops of intestines around the heart stared back at me. My mind had been so set on cancer that I had failed to take a proper history from the owner. I knew that I had not asked about possible trauma, like being hit by a car. Dashing into the exam room, I breathlessly asked if there was any way his dog could have been run over. Even though he lived on a dirt road, the owner testified that people generally drove too fast on the long, straight stretch in front of his house. It made sense now... This was a ruptured diaphragm from being hit by a vehicle! The dog still had to have risky emergency surgery to repair the tear in the diaphragm, which allowed the intestines to enter the chest cavity, but the chances of survival were drastically improved compared to my erroneous initial diagnosis of metastatic cancer. After the challenging task of suturing the torn diaphragm, my patient recovered quite well and was breathing normally. This dog would survive after all...

"...And I feel sick that I almost convinced

the owner that euthanasia was the best option. Mrs. Jones, this job will knock me down pretty hard at times."

Mrs. Jones cleared her throat, and a stern look came across her face. "You will make mistakes, Andrew, but it does not mean that you are not an excellent, caring vet. We are not perfect. Keep your head held high, and believe in yourself. And do remember, that dog is alive because of your attentiveness and surgical skills."

Mrs. Jones had a way of talking with conviction. She had the wisdom that I sought. What a contradiction she was: physically frail and weak, but spiritually and emotionally so powerful. When she spoke, I listened.

After we had finished eating supper, Leigh and I helped clean the kitchen and put away the leftovers, as usual. Mrs. Jones hummed softly as she cleaned, occasionally singing the lyrics of a hymn quietly.

Jetta, tail wagging furiously, awaited my arrival at the couch where she anticipated my being face to face with her on the floor. Soon, I was attempting to dodge her licking tongue on my nose as I reached for the basket underneath the sofa. Wiping my face with my sleeve, I peered up at Mrs. Jones who was slapping her knee and laughing.

"Miss Priss is good at planting her kisses right on the mark!" She chuckled.

I just shook my head, stifling a laugh.

I walked to the dining table and dumped the contents of the leather game case on top. Time began to vanish peacefully.

I thought of the fragile redbud blooms outside the house. In a short two weeks, the purple blossoms would be gone. My mind drifted. Like the redbud flower, we are only in this life a brief while. How beautiful life can be; the beauty is enhanced by its brevity. As quickly as a moment is born, it belongs to the past and becomes a memory, and these memories are often what we appreciate even more than the actual moments because the memories last.

I glanced to my left at my wife and thought about how Leigh and I were both young with so much life ahead of us. I then looked across the table at Mrs. Jones and realized that not long ago Mrs. Jones was young, too.

"Oops, Andrew!" Mrs. Jones was smiling. "Looks like you were daydreaming again. You missed your chance. I guess I will have to put down my 7 and 8 where you should have."

I smiled back as I watched Mrs. Jones capitalize on my mistake.

We played on until 10 o'clock when the

echoing grandfather clock in the other room reminded us of our "mortality." Mrs. Jones pushed her way up to her feet and said, "I have a little gift for y'all out in the garage. Come, right this way."

Leigh and I followed Mrs. Jones out the kitchen door, down the three breezeway steps, and into the garage. There, just under the pitter patter of doggie feet sign sat two small plastic pots with what appeared to be frail twigs poking out of the dirt. I scratched my head attempting to figure out what they might be.

"I told you I would give you some of my baby elm trees that volunteered in my flower bed." Mrs. Jones bent down slowly to pick up one of the pots. "These two are offsprings from my favorite elm tree right out by my driveway." She paused, looking down at her gift. "It will amaze you just how fast these little saplings will turn into full-grown trees in your yard. And remember, be sure to plant them where you would like to create a shady spot."

Nodding my head, I imagined what the two trees would look like in my yard one day.

Mrs. Jones softly touched the tiny plant in her hand. "I just love an elm tree. I know you will too…."

CHAPTER 6: "ANSWER TO MY PRAYERS"

I parked my truck in its usual spot beneath the favorite elm tree, but the timing was much different, for the sun was just beginning to turn the eastern sky on this spring day. Jetta was my priority. Mrs. Jones had called me an hour earlier to say that Jetta had vomited all afternoon the day before and through the night. Anxiously, I drove the half hour to her house to examine the problem.

Up went the noisy garage door, and out stepped Mrs. Jones cradling her little dog in the low light of dawn.

"I am just worried sick about my Jetta," she said, obviously fighting back tears.

"Let me take her in to the clinic and see what I can do for her," I offered as optimistically as I could.

Carefully scooping Jetta from Mrs. Jones's arms, I placed her in the front seat of my truck. Though lethargic, Jetta still mustered enough energy to lick me in the face and give a few short tail wags.

Before getting in my truck, I gave Mrs. Jones

a long hug. "I will do everything I can for Jetta."

She just nodded and stared back at me, her lips trembling.

I hopped into my truck, slowly backed out of the short driveway onto 12th street and looked at Mrs. Jones who still stood by her elm tree waving goodbye. I knew I had to get Jetta feeling better.

Once at the veterinary clinic, I immediately began my physical exam. Jetta was subdued, and it hurt me to see the normally energetic dog now lethargic. Her gums were pink; her heart and lungs were clear; her temperature was normal. But then a "knot" formed in my stomach when my hand palpated her abdomen. A feeling of despair rushed through me as my fingers touched the borders of another "knot," yet this one was real.

"Oh no," I mumbled to myself. "Let's get an X-ray on Jetta," I suggested rather frantically to my technician.

Obediently, Jetta allowed me to roll her on her side and then her back to obtain the views I needed. I nervously stepped around the corner to the digital viewing screen and held my breath.

The radiograph showed what I already knew. In her central abdomen was a round tumor nearly the size of a baseball. There was no denying that it was a growth and that Jetta would need surgery for a proper diagnosis.

Swallowing hard to clear my throat, I called Mrs. Jones, and she answered on the first ring.

"Hey, Mrs. Jones," my voice was low and shaky. I struggled to say the words I had to say. "So, I did an X-ray on Jetta, and I found something concerning…" I paused, but Mrs. Jones did not speak. I continued, "I believe she has a tumor in her abdomen. I'm not sure what it's attached to, but I can find out." I swallowed hard again and cleared my throat. "We need to do an exploratory surgery. Are you ok with that?"

For a few seconds Mrs. Jones did not make a sound. Then, she responded in a surprisingly strong voice, "Do what you have to do, Andrew. I trust you completely and know that you will look after Jetta like she's your own. I love that sweet, little doggie so much." Her voice wavered. "I will be praying for you and Jetta…. Oh and, Andrew?"

"Yes ma'am?" I responded quietly.

"If it looks too bad in there, too aggressive, then I do not want her to wake up. I want her to go peacefully."

"Are you sure, Mrs. Jones?" But I knew she was right.

"Yes, Andrew, I'm sure. I want what's best for Jetta, and I have so many wonderful memories with her."

"Let's hope for the best," I said, trying to

retain some optimism.

"Bye bye, Andrew. I love you."

"I love you too, Mrs. Jones."

After checking Jetta's preanesthetic bloodwork, which looked unremarkable, I started prepping her for surgery— IV catheter, fluids, sedation, induction, monitoring equipment. Jetta was positioned on her back as we shaved her abdominal fur and applied the surgical scrub to her pigmented skin. Slipping on my sterile gloves, I opened my surgical pack, placed the drapes across her body, and lifted the scalpel blade in my right hand. I stole a quick look at the bird feeder hanging outside the window and drew a deep breath. Moment of truth. I knew that Mrs. Jones was praying. The world outside the window continued without concern for anyone's feelings. The cars sped down the street. The birds chirped and pecked at the seeds in the feeder. Dogs barked loudly in the yard. The sun shone brightly. But my job was here in this room. I focused on my surgical field and delicately pressed the new scalpel blade to Jetta's tender underside.

The blade effortlessly sliced through Jetta's skin near her belly button. The next incision found its way deeper through the linea where the abdominal muscles joined in the center. I was in.

Drawing another deep breath and exhaling

slowly, I feared looking inside, the unknown twisting my thoughts. Sifting through the intestines, my hands grasped the object of my mission. There in the omentum, the fat that surrounds the intestines, I saw it... but could it really be?

Relief flooded my anxious emotions. Jetta was going to be ok after all!

Staring back at me from the open incision was a lipoma, a harmless wad of encapsulated fat. Nothing more. To be certain, my fingers worked their way over all major structures to ensure that I was not missing anything else. How interesting that a lipoma should be located in this area. Never had I seen one in the omentum, nor have I seen one since. Aside from the slippery nature of fat, removal was easy, and I began suturing the incision closed.

I kept Jetta on the surgery table until she swallowed several times, removed her endotracheal tube from her airway, and cradled her in my blanketed arms to transport her to a recovery kennel. Lining the cage with extra blankets and a heating pad, I sat longer than I usually did with my postoperative patients.

After confirming that Jetta was comfortable, I closed the kennel door quietly and made my way to the office. I imagined Mrs. Jones fretting by her phone alone in her house, so I quickly dialed her number.

"Mrs. Jones," I said happily with a huge smile on my face. She knew immediately from my tone.

"Oh, Andrew, you have good news!" She exclaimed.

"I surely do!"

After explaining the procedure, I surmised to Mrs. Jones that Jetta must have contracted a virus to upset her stomach, and we had incidentally discovered the lipoma mass while searching for the cause of the vomiting. Whatever the case, I felt highly confident that her vomiting ailment was not life threatening. The plan would be to hospitalize Jetta overnight on IV fluids and anti-vomiting medication.

"You just don't know how happy this makes me," Mrs. Jones sang.

Oh, but I did know. I pictured Mrs. Jones on the other end of the line, sitting in her chair smiling as all her Beanie Babies peered down from high on the walls.

"This is an answer to my prayers, Andrew."

This I knew too. Jetta was more than a black poodle. She was a soul companion to an 83-year-old widow. Perhaps the little dog gave her owner the motivation to keep going in life, a life that was full of physical and emotional obstacles. And what an impact the two were making in my life.

"I will take her to you tomorrow when I leave work," I said. "I bet she will feel just fine by then."

"And I will have supper waiting on you, ok?"

"Aw, Mrs. Jones, that sounds great, but you don't have to. Let me bring something to eat when I come."

"No sir-ee. You just bring yourself and your pretty wife if she can come. See you tomorrow, Andrew. Oh, what a wonderful day!"

I hung up the phone on the desk, spun around in my chair, and looked at a small Carolina wren pecking seeds from the bird feeder suspended on the other side of the window. The sun was shining brightly. The sky was deep blue. The longleaf pine branches swayed gently. Life carried on.

It was going to be a good day.

A few days after Jetta's surgery, with the little dog safely back home with Mrs. Jones, I turned into my sandy driveway at the end of an exhausting work day; it had been long, hard, and aggravating. Many days in the vet field are. I was in a bit of a pessimistic mood, thinking about a case that had gone poorly, and my mind was drained as

I distractedly steered my truck into the yard. The days were getting longer, and I was happy at least to be arriving home before dark. A gopher tortoise watched me from the mouth of its burrow and brought a slight smile to my tense face before I parked and exited the truck.

A package on the front steps to my house caught my eye. I walked over, picked up the box, and spun it around to view the return address. A larger smile formed on my lips. Sitting tiredly on the steps, I opened the package with my pocketknife and discovered a handwritten gold card and a small figurine of a doctor with arms outstretched skyward.

Dear Andrew—
When I saw this doctor figurine, it made me think of you lifting up your hands in prayer, that God would be with you and Jetta during the time of surgery. You are a man of faith, and my prayer is that you always will show God's love regardless of what and whom you have to deal with. Always remember that I, plus Jetta, love and appreciate your life and what you have done for us.

Love and tell Leigh hello for me.
Frances Jones   5/28/14

Raising my teary eyes from the note, I stared across my yard. The gopher tortoise was still there on the edge of the wood line reminding me of God's care for all of His creatures.

    Maybe it was a good day after all.

CHAPTER 7: "THE KEY IS TO BE CONTENT DURING THE HARD TIMES"

Usually, I planned our visits in advance, to allow Mrs. Jones time to prepare for company in her home since she loved to cook. But today was different. It was nearly 7:30 in the evening, and I had worked all day without much of a break. I was also on call, carrying the emergency phone in my pocket. Before leaving the clinic, I dialed Mrs. Jones's number.

"Hey, Mrs. Jones. Do you mind if I stop by for a little bit? I'm on call tonight and just need a break. I could use some good company, too," I forced a weary laugh.

"Oh, Andrew, of course you can come by. Stay as long as you want. Honey, you don't ever have to ask. Just drop in when you want."

I mindlessly drove the five minutes to her house, attempting to clear the stressors in my head. The exhaustion of the day, and week, had caught up to me. I desperately needed a place to unwind. My truck seemed to automatically carry me to East 12th Street where the simple, single story, stone-façade house with the elm tree and cosmos awaited me.

Slowly rolling to a stop, I saw the garage door lift open. Mrs. Jones was watching like she always did.

A few minutes later, I found myself inside the house on the plush sofa with Mrs. Jones and Jetta sitting to my right. In my hand was a glass of ice water. I took a sip and then exhaled slowly, rubbing my temple with my left hand.

"You look worn out, Andrew. Poor thing. I know your profession demands a lot of you. But just stay strong. You don't realize the impact you have on people through your work. You are trained to help and serve others. I believe God called you to do this job." Mrs. Jones looked to her left out the bay window at the waning August light. "Life is not easy. It's not supposed to be. Without struggles, how else can a person grow in faith and character?"

Here was a twice-widowed lady riddled with health concerns, and yet she was encouraging *me* to stay focused and optimistic.

Looking startled, she asked. "Andrew, have you eaten supper yet? Oh dear! I am so sorry I didn't check before now."

I had not eaten anything since a sandwich for lunch, so I slowly shook my head. "No, but it's ok. I will pick up something to eat when I leave here in a little while. I just needed to sit down and clear my head first."

"No, no, absolutely not!" She rebuked me. "I have some leftovers in the fridge. Come, sit at the table. I'm going to heat you up a plate."

I tried to object as she struggled to her feet. "Mrs. Jones, thank you but…"

"Uh-ah," she said wagging a stern finger at me. "Don't argue. I'm getting you a plate."

I followed obediently to the kitchen as she opened the refrigerator door.

"Hmmm, let's see. I have this grilled chicken. Oh, and this pasta salad. Green beans too. It might be a hodge-podge meal, but it should fill you up," she turned and grinned.

"I'm not picky, Mrs. Jones. Honestly, I feel like I can eat anything right now," I admitted.

"Do sit. I will get your plate ready," she commanded.

Typically, I would refuse to sit while Mrs. Jones was on her feet, but this time I assented.

With her back to me, Mrs. Jones suggested, "Why don't you tell me about something you enjoy doing? Get your mind off the stressful workday."

I thought for a few seconds. "I don't think I have told you that I enjoy knife making, right?"

"No, you have not." Mrs. Jones responded.

"What a fascinating activity," she turned to face me as she spoke.

I continued, "Well, a few years ago, I decided that I wanted to try to make a knife with an antler handle. I was introduced to a man about your age who has made knives for years, and he specifically loves antler-handle knives. He lives over in Carnegie, Georgia, about two hours or so from here. It's tough to get over there as much as I would like to, but I try to go about once a month."

"And I bet he loves having you over," Mrs. Jones added. "You have a way of showing old people like me that we still matter."

"I don't think you understand how much I enjoy our visits and how much I learn from you." I spoke emphatically. "Like you told me before, we should all make time to celebrate the wisdom of age."

"When you get old like me, you begin to realize that you should have done more listening than speaking," Mrs. Jones said while letting out a laugh. "I'm pretty outspoken and opinionated, but the one thing that has kept me grounded is God. I would not have made it this far without His hand to hold. So, tell me, what do you do when you go to see this man? What's his name?"

"His name is Mr. Andrews, and what a role model he is to me. He reminds me of my mom's dad, who passed away twelve years ago," I said, drifting into my memories. "What began as tutorials on how to make a knife, quickly turned into fun visits with Mr. Andrews. We fish. We cook. We sit and talk about life. It's so relaxing to go there, the same as coming here to see you. I get to step out of the fast pace of life for a short while and just enjoy being in the moment."

"I'm so happy I can offer that kind of feeling to you too," Mrs. Jones said smiling. "It's important to do things you enjoy, especially when you have a hectic lifestyle. Life's all about figuring out how to balance. There is no single right way to do it because everyone's situation is different. The key is to be content during the hard times, believing that it will get better, that God will see you through your trials."

Grinning, I replied in more of a joking tone, "I'm still trying to find that balance, Mrs. Jones!"

"You are already ahead of the game, Andrew. You are trying, and that's worth a lot more than you can imagine. In fact, you will never be able to find perfect balance in this life. It's all about trying and having a positive attitude. Face your troubles head on."

Mrs. Jones peered down at Jetta who was resting at her feet and then spun around to the counter and said, "Let me get your supper ready first. Then we can continue our talk."

She opened the microwave to set my plate of cold food inside and pressed the settings. While my food warmed, she asked, "Would you like some biscuits, too?"

"I surely would, if you have some." The mention of biscuits triggered my thoughts of jelly. "Do you have any jelly? I love putting jelly on biscuits."

"I love jellies too, Andrew," she said opening the refrigerator door. "Oh yes, let me see. I have grape, strawberry, blackberry, and mayhaw. Which would you prefer?"

"How about mayhaw?" I responded, licking my lips. "Have you ever tried pepper jelly before?" I asked.

"Yes, certainly. I haven't had some in years, but I really like it. Good pepper jelly is more difficult to find these days," she said, shaking her head.

"Well, coincidentally, my friend Mr. Andrews makes some fine pepper jelly. Actually, we have some on crackers with cream cheese every time I go to his house. Literally, every time. It's one of our rituals," I laughed. "I had never had any before I ate his."

"Where does he get his peppers from, do you know?" Mrs. Jones inquired.

"He grows them in big pots in his yard."

"I would love to try some of his. Could you get me some?"

"Absolutely! Next time I go to his house," I answered excitedly. I knew Mr. Andrews would be proud to share his homemade jelly.

The microwave chimed, and Mrs. Jones placed the mayhaw jelly in front of me on the table. She then grabbed my plate of food and set it next to the jelly.

"Would you like sweet tea or water tonight, honey?"

"Water will be fine. Thank you."

After refilling my glass of ice water, Mrs. Jones heated two biscuits in the microwave, handed them to me, and sat down in her chair at the dinner table across from me.

"Andrew, you are a fine, young man. Continue up the path you are on and never lose sight of what guides you, my dear." She smiled sweetly. "Will you please say the blessing?"

"Yes ma'am, of course."

After I said the blessing over my meal, I anticipated Mrs. Jones's usual question about interesting veterinary cases, but this time she talked of other topics. She knew that my workday had been intense and probably assumed that I did not want to discuss veterinary medicine tonight.

"This August heat and drought have really done a number on my plants. I feel like they need watering every day, except those hardy cosmos. Did you see them out front?" She pointed a bent, bony finger toward the front of the house. "They are so resilient. Remind me, and I will give you some seeds before you leave. You can scatter them now or wait until the spring, but if you throw them out now, be sure you water them to get them growing."

I nodded my head. "I would love to have some. Thank you."

"I can tell that you have quite a green thumb," Mrs. Jones said. "You appreciate nature, and that says a lot about who you are." With a reminiscing look she spoke again: "I have always loved gardening. As you know, I can't get outside like I used to, but of course I still love doing a little here and there in my flower beds."

Chewing slowly on a bite of pasta salad, I was suddenly jarred out of the conversation by the emergency phone buzzing furiously in my pocket.

"Uh-oh, Mrs. Jones. This might mean I have to leave. An emergency call just came through," I said pulling the phone from my pocket to view the screen.

"You remember, now, that you have a gift. The ability to help. Don't let the down moments of the job keep you down. March forward with faith in knowing that you are on the path that you were meant to travel."

I nodded my head. "Thank you, Mrs. Jones."

Hurriedly, I finished eating my supper before returning the call. I walked to the den, sat on the couch, and dialed the number.

"Hey, this is Dr. Curtis, I just got your emergency call."

The voice on the other end of the line made me smile because it sounded like Mrs. Jones.

"Oh, thank you so much for calling me back. I'm not sure if this justifies as an emergency visit, but I don't want to ignore any signs," the lady said softly. "My little dog, Precious, has thrown up three times within the hour. She has never done this before."

Glancing over my shoulder at Mrs. Jones who was cleaning my dishes in the sink, I felt a surge of desire to help the concerned lady and her vomiting dog.

"Why don't we go ahead and have a look tonight, you know, just to be sure nothing major is going on with Precious. And if nothing else, I can give her a shot for nausea," I spoke in a reassuring tone.

"Are you sure you don't mind? It would definitely make me feel better," the elderly woman said appreciatively.

"Yes ma'am. I really don't mind at all. See you in a few minutes."

I stood from the couch and walked to the kitchen where Mrs. Jones had finished cleaning the dishes, table, and counter.

"Looks like duty calls, Mrs. Jones. Thank you so much for feeding me and talking to me. Your words really have a way of lifting me up."

Mrs. Jones smiled widely and hugged my neck. "You come back now, and do tell your pretty wife I said 'hello.'"

"I will, Mrs. Jones," I said, kneeling to pat Jetta goodbye.

The night air was sticky and oppressively hot, typical of August in South Georgia, but I felt refreshed. Walking to my truck, I touched the elm tree's bark and looked up. Through the leaves, I could see a crescent moon nearly overhead. I smiled at the thought of the mood change in me from an hour before. All thanks to Mrs. Jones!

CHAPTER 8: "THANKSGIVING"

The sun had risen above the treetops in a cloudless sky, but the air still held a cool dampness of dawn. I pulled down the short driveway under the bright yellow elm tree. No need to turn my truck off this time. Mrs. Jones was already out waiting in front of her garage.

With the window down, I called out, "Happy Thanksgiving, Mrs. Jones!"

"And a Happy Thanksgiving to you too, Andrew!" She responded, clapping her hands together.

She was dressed in bright colors with flowers on her sweater. Her short hair was recently styled, and she had makeup on her face. On her neck a silver necklace hung down with a small, silver cross charm attached.

Eagerly hopping out of my truck, I hugged Mrs. Jones and helped her up into the passenger seat.

"I'm going to leave Jetta inside while we go eat. She will be fine for a few hours, don't you think? I told her to guard the house!" Mrs. Jones said humorously.

"Yes ma'am. I think she will be just fine," I

grinned in reply.

As we rode east, Mrs. Jones was in high spirits, and we talked the whole half-hour drive to Alapaha. She wanted to know as much as she could about my in-laws, whom she was going to meet. Pulling off the quiet, country road, I steered down my long, sandy driveway, past the longleaf pines.

"You have a beautiful spot here, Andrew. I'm so glad I get to finally see where you live out here by the Alapaha River." Mrs. Jones eyed her surroundings, nodding in approval. Then her eyes met the cosmos, which had come up from the seeds she had given me. "Look at those. Look at those! You decided to go ahead and plant them for the fall. Why wait, right? They look wonderful there. I do absolutely love cosmos!"

"I love them, too, Mrs. Jones. Thank you for sharing them with us." I stared proudly at my pretty fall flower bed not yet killed by the cold and brought my truck to a stop.

The front door to my house opened, and Leigh and her family came out to greet us in the yard. Leigh's parents had driven the short distance from Douglas, Georgia, while Leigh's sister and her husband had flown from Austin, Texas, for the holiday.

Mrs. Jones was the first to speak. "Hello, y'all! This is delightful to get the chance to meet you folks! You sure have raised a fine girl in Leigh."

After the introductions, I led Mrs. Jones slowly up our steps and into our home. The fresh smells filled the room from my mother-in-law's cooking. I had optimistic expectations that pet owners this day would be basking in the spirit of the special holiday and that no emergency situation could possibly arise during mealtime. It was too pretty of a day to be pulled away. It was, after all, Thanksgiving Day.

I was still standing in the entrance of my home when I felt it... the dreaded emergency phone buzzing impatiently on my belt, wrestling me away from the peaceful gathering.

I quickly excused myself, walked outside into the bright sunlight, and dialed the number.

"Hey, this is Dr. Curtis returning your call."

"Yeah, you need to see my dog right now. He broke his leg. Can't put any weight on it." The deep, gruff voice was demanding.

"Ok, I see. Is he crying out in pain?"

"Well, no, but he's obviously in pain. I told you he broke his leg. Wouldn't you be in pain?" The man's voice was beginning to angrily rise in volume.

I could sense the sarcasm but remained calm. "If he's not miserable, then I can recommend that you give some pain medicine that you might have at home to hold him over until after Thanksgiving lunch."

"I will NOT wait. I want you to see us right NOW!" The man's voice became high pitched with rage.

"Are you by chance a regular client of ours?"

"No, I'm not, but that shouldn't matter! I can't believe you are trying to blow this off. He could need surgery if it's a bad break, and I want the surgery done TODAY!" He fumed.

"Well, sir, even if it is broken and requires surgery, it won't be done today. I can splint it until we can get time to do the surgery..."

"This is unbelievable!" He interrupted. "You are the most unprofessional veterinarian I have ever talked to! I don't need you!"

The man hung up on me. Not even a "Happy Thanksgiving" or "Sorry to bother you on Thanksgiving." I was not trying to make him mad, but if the dog could have waited for two hours, with pain medicine, before I had a look, then I could have enjoyed my Thanksgiving meal. And, I was unsure that the dog actually did have a leg fracture. Many times when an owner suspects a broken bone, it is not.

The sun was still shining, but my mood was dampened. My head hung low as I entered my house, and I told Mrs. Jones of the poor conversation I had just experienced.

"Mrs. Jones, some people just don't understand," I said, staring at the floor. "I try to treat everyone fairly and give the best advice I can..."

Hand on my forearm and a serious look on her face, Mrs. Jones said, "Andrew, do not let anyone convince you that you are not a caring person. You ARE caring! It's who you are, and you shouldn't change a thing about you."

My mother-in-law was placing the food on the table when my emergency phone buzzed again. I couldn't believe it. Hopes sinking, I excused myself a second time and went outside to return the call.

"Hey, it's Dr. Curtis, just returning your call." I knew my voice sounded defeated.

"I really hate to bother you like this on Thanksgiving, but I just don't know what to do." The woman's voice on the other end sounded sincere and grateful. Her humble tone enlivened my willing spirit.

"It's ok. What's going on?" I asked, a little more attentively.

"My little twelve-year-old dachshund just ate our entire chocolate cake. I really wish I didn't have to bother you like this... I just don't know what to do."

"You did the right thing by calling. Are you a regular client? Do you know where the clinic is?"

"Yes sir, we have used y'all for years."

"I'm going to leave right now. Takes me about 30 minutes to get there, but I'm on my way," I said making my way up the stairs to my house to report the situation.

"I cannot thank you enough, Dr. Curtis. See you soon."

So gracious. That was all I needed, someone who appreciated my service. I was eager to help this woman.

"Hey y'all," I called out, poking my head inside through the open doorway. "Looks like I have an emergency that I will have to see. Shouldn't take too long. Go ahead and eat, and I will be back in an hour and a half."

Mrs. Jones was the first to speak. "Oh dear, Andrew. I am sorry you have to leave now. But I guess that's all part of what you do. Your job is one of great service."

Nodding my head with a smile, I shut the door behind me.

Once at the clinic, I met the woman with her dog in the parking lot and took them inside the building. I immediately induced vomiting, and the engorged dachshund let out a volcanic expulsion of the chocolatey ingesta. The dog's owner, a middle-aged woman, continued to express her appreciation of my work, and it felt good. These were the cases I longed for: a grateful owner with a successfully treated pet.

I cheerfully drove my route back home and gazed at the gorgeous cotton field in the sunshine with the colorful yellow poplars and red maple trees in the hardwood bottom beyond. House after house had cars lined up in the driveways. So many others were enjoying the holiday with their families. And now, I was headed back to mine.

As I pulled into my driveway, I rolled the windows of my truck down to draw in the late fall air. I could see the bright orange cosmos by my house swaying in the breeze, welcoming me back home.

Entering my house once more, Mrs. Jones clapped her hands together. "And how is the little doggie, Andrew? Did you get it feeling better?"

"I believe so," I said nodding my head. "Seems my patient had too much dessert. Got into the chocolate cake!"

Mrs. Jones let out a laugh and ushered me to the dining table.

Uninterrupted by any more emergency calls for the next hour and a half, I enjoyed my Thanksgiving meal and relished my company's presence in my home. The time finally came to take Mrs. Jones back to Tifton and for me to do afternoon treatments at the clinic. Mrs. Jones said her goodbyes reluctantly, and even though none of us wanted the afternoon to end, the departure was not sad.

On our way down the driveway, Mrs. Jones peered out the truck window and said, "I know what those are."

Her finger pointed at two small plants in the yard, no more than a foot and half tall, with pine straw mulch encircling the trunks and orange flagging ribbon tied on a branch each.

"I told you that you are going to love the elms I gave you...."

CHAPTER 9: "THE DIAGNOSIS"

589. Not the number I wanted to see. Certainly not pertaining to Jetta's glucose reading. All the signs were present, and now I stared at the proof... diabetes. Mrs. Jones's little Jetta had diabetes.

My head spun at the realization that this would be a tough situation for a widowed woman in her 80s with her own long list of medical problems. The dilemma— twice daily insulin injections with periodic blood sugar checks. Not only that, but the insulin syringes are notoriously small and difficult to read, especially for someone battling the progressive eye disease of macular degeneration like Mrs. Jones was. "How could she possibly do it?" I thought.

I called Mrs. Jones.

"Mrs. Jones, I found out why Jetta has been drinking so much water and why she has had urinary accidents in the house." I took a deep breath and spilled forth the answer: "She has diabetes..."

Pausing for a few seconds allowing the news to settle, I continued, "It is treatable, but... well... she will need insulin injections... every day… twice a day."

Again, silence on the other end of the phone.

"Mrs. Jones?"

"Yes, I'm here… I guess I have got to do it for my little Priss. I don't really have much of a choice," she reasoned.

"Ok, Mrs. Jones, I will explain it all in more detail later, but let me keep her here for a few days to see if I can get her blood sugar regulated first. When she is ready to go, I will take her to you and show you how to give the insulin shots."

"Do you think she will be alright, Andrew?"

"I do. I really do. I think we can get her feeling better." In my mind I was hoping that the words I just spoke were true. Diabetes in a pet can be a challenging illness.

"Thank you, Andrew. I will be praying for you and Jetta."

After three days of repeatedly checking Jetta's blood glucose and adjusting her insulin dose, I was prepared to triumphantly return Jetta to Mrs. Jones. There was a sparkle in those little eyes, an apparent appreciation for my care, as I placed Jetta into the front seat of my truck.

The quick, familiar drive to Mrs. Jones's house produced mounting excitement inside me, and I smiled as I pulled down the short driveway to park by the elm tree. The old house looked quiet.

To the west, the cloudy evening sky had turned a blaze orange with zigzags of purple streaks. One pocket in the clouds opened to allow a glimpse of pale blue sky beyond with visible rays of inviting light peeking through. There, at the top of the elm tree, a sliver of the late sun's orange glow fell on a cluster of leaves. I felt a reassurance at the sight, the timing just right.

The house abruptly came to life as the garage door sprang open. Out stepped Mrs. Jones slowly making her way to me with a wide smile spread across her face.

"Oh, my Jetta! I have missed you so much."

Holding the wiggly dog up to lick Mrs. Jones in her face, I soaked in the happiness. I then carried Jetta through the garage and glanced at the sign by the breezeway door.

NO HOME IS COMPLETE WITHOUT THE PITTER PATTER OF DOGGIE FEET.

Once inside the kitchen, I coached Mrs. Jones on the process of giving the insulin injections. Over and over, she practiced drawing up the insulin into the tiny syringe, the amount a minuscule three units. This small quantity took concentration on even my experienced behalf, but imagine the patience required for an elderly woman with rheumatoid arthritis who had never before used a syringe and who had to attempt to see through the blinding effects of her macular degeneration. Despite all her health problems, Mrs. Jones did not complain.

"Wow, Mrs. Jones, you are getting the hang of it," I said with genuine awe in my voice.

She looked up at me and laughed: "I have to do it for my Jetta."

Next, I instructed her to sit in one of her dining chairs with Jetta's food bowl between her feet. As Jetta ravenously pounced on her food, I showed Mrs. Jones how she could lean forward in her seated position, grasp the loose skin behind Jetta's shoulder blades, and administer the shot while Jetta was distractedly eating.

"Nice job, Mrs. Jones!" I said, thoroughly impressed. "Do you feel comfortable with that technique?"

"I do, Andrew. Maybe I will be able to treat Miss Priss Tail after all," she said sighing deeply and pushing herself up from the chair.

Mrs. Jones, of course, had supper prepared-- black eyed peas, mashed potatoes, and pork chops that she had gotten on sale from Sav A Lot. She was always proud of the bargains she found, a result, no doubt, of growing up during the Great Depression.

"I will serve your plate," she insisted as she

piled on the food.

I jumped to my feet. "No, Mrs. Jones, I will fix mine. You don't have to."

"Ah ah ah," she wagged a finger at me. "Sit back down. It's my treat."

I laughed and sat back down.

Setting my dinner in front of me, she made her plate of food and took her seat across from me.

"Andrew, will you please say the blessing?"

"Of course I will, Mrs. Jones."

We bowed our heads and closed our eyes as I prayed and gave my thanks.

Mrs. Jones opened her eyes, reached for her napkin, and asked, "Any other interesting vet cases, besides Jetta?"

I thought for a few seconds. "One case comes to mind. Happened a few weeks back, and it involves insulin…"

…Slurring her words terribly, the pet owner sounded as confused as I was. Did I hear her correctly? Surely she was out of her mind and could not possibly mean what she was saying. I asked again, "65 units?" Her reply was the same, a definitive "yes." I shook my head in disbelief. The client with which I was speaking informed me that she, the client, was a diabetic and became confused when her blood sugar dropped. After the client drew up her whopping insulin dose to give to herself, her tiny pet chihuahua, weighing a measly

four pounds, hopped into her lap. Without thinking, this lady had injected her human insulin dose into her dog (which, by the way, was NOT diabetic). Now, the owner changed her story, saying that she did not think she injected her dog. "You better bring your little dog to me so I can check her out thoroughly... just in case. Oh, and do you have someone to drive you here?" I inquired, trying not to be too offensive, but I knew this lady was not in her right mind to be driving a car. True to her word, the owner had found a relative to bring her to the vet clinic, and upon arrival, the tiny chihuahua looked perfectly fine. I was beginning to think all was ok and that the owner had imagined giving the injection. However, when I performed a precautionary blood glucose check on the tiny specimen, I was shocked to see the reading was 54, which was definitely below the normal range. I placed an IV catheter into the arm of my new patient to be prepared in case I should need quick intravenous access. After a few more minutes, I rechecked the blood glucose... 48! No question about it now. This dog did indeed receive an insulin dose. I was still unclear exactly how much because I did not know if the owner was remembering correctly, but she kept saying "65 units." Also, I had learned that this was not just any insulin, but a potent, long-acting type that we do not use in veterinary medicine. How long would the effects last at that high of a dose in a four-

pound miniature dog? I was uncertain of the answer, but I did know one thing. This dog needed a constant rate IV dextrose (sugar) drip to maintain an appropriate blood glucose level, since insulin lowers the blood's glucose. One day turned to two, and two days turned to three. Each time I attempted to wean the little dog off the dextrose drip, her blood sugar plummeted. While on the IVs, though, she felt normal and spunky. Finally, on day five of treatment, I crossed my fingers as I had done the previous days and began slowing the drip rate. Her blood sugar was holding steady! I discontinued the treatment, watched her closely, and kept her at the hospital one additional day to be sure she did not regress. In the end, all was well with the tiny chihuahua, and she experienced no lasting effects from her accidental injection of the largest insulin dose I have ever heard of in a dog...

"And just think, Jetta here is three or four times the size of that little doggie you treated, and she only needs three units," Mrs. Jones said, shaking her head in wonder.

"Yes ma'am. Insulin is a mighty powerful hormone as you can see," I responded.

"I just love these stories, Andrew. You do have a fascinating job," Mrs. Jones said, "even if it can be terribly stressful."

After supper and once the dishes were cleaned, Mrs. Jones said proudly, "Let me show you Jetta's bedtime routine. I am going to put her to bed a little earlier tonight. Poor thing must be exhausted. Been in the hospital for three days."

Jetta looked up quizzically at her owner, cocked her head to the side, and whined excitedly.

"Let's go to bed, Jetta," Mrs. Jones commanded with a swift wave of her hand.

Down the picture-lined hallway, Jetta led us to the master bedroom. On the left-hand side of the room next to the dresser sat a tan dog crate. Jetta energetically pranced inside and stuck her head back out.

"She's waiting on her treat," Mrs. Jones grinned, slowly bending over to offer the cookie.

Gingerly grasping the treat in her mouth, Jetta disappeared to the back of the crate while Mrs. Jones simply draped a small white towel over the opening.

"You don't even shut the door?" I asked, surprised.

"Sure don't. I just hang this towel over the entrance, and she stays in there all night. Never even a whimper to get out." Mrs. Jones smiled down at the crate on the floor: "Night night, my sweet Jetta. I love you."

We walked back into the den, and Mrs.

Jones asked, "Do you have time to play some Rummikub?"

"I think I can make time to play a few games," I joked. She knew I loved to play.

Rummikub at that old dining table held a special power over me. It transformed any worries I might have had of the future into comfortable feelings of purpose.

As we played, we chatted like we always would, allowing time to slip away from us... until the old grandfather clock in the next room brought us back to present time.

We rose from the table, and Mrs. Jones put a finger quickly into the air and said, "Wait a minute. I have been meaning to give you a key to my house." She shuffled her way to a side table drawer by the couch. "It will make me feel better. In case I need you, you can always get inside. And besides, I want you to feel free to come and go like it's your own house."

Taking the gold key tethered to a purple ribbon, I hugged Mrs. Jones and stepped out into the dark breezeway. "See you soon, Mrs. Jones."

"Bye bye, honey. I appreciate you... more than you know."

The following day, Leigh and I sent Mrs. Jones a bouquet of flowers. Three days later, we received a card in the mail. The front of the card pictured a painting of a small wren with Mrs. Jones's handwritten note on the inside.

> *Dear Andrew and Leigh:*
> *You are special to me—*
> *The flowers are beautiful, and I really appreciate your thoughtfulness, <u>but</u> I want only to see you and fellowship with you— you need your money! Both of you are tops in my book, and I love and thank you.*
> *Frances*

CHAPTER 10: "WHAT CAN MAKE A RELATIONSHIP SO STRONG"

"Andrew, Jetta has begun wetting in the house again. Do you think we should check her sugar?"

I paused before answering. It had been several months since Jetta's diabetes diagnosis, and up to this point she had been responding quite well to the insulin injections.

"Yes ma'am," I answered optimistically into the phone. "Let's check her tomorrow. Don't feed her breakfast in the morning, and don't give her insulin either. She still acts like she feels ok, right? Still eating well?"

"Yes, yes. She acts as spunky as ever and eats like a horse!" Mrs. Jones said through a chuckle.

"All right then. I will swing by on my way to work tomorrow and keep her for the day to check her out."

"Oh, thank you, Andrew. You just don't know how much I appreciate this."

"I'm happy to help, Mrs. Jones. See you tomorrow."

"Oh yeah, and don't you worry about

supper tomorrow. I will cook you up something tasty. Please see if Leigh can come eat with us too."

"Yes ma'am," I responded, smiling to myself. I no longer objected to her cooking for me.

The following morning at daylight, I pulled into her driveway. Before I could turn off my truck, the garage door opened, and Mrs. Jones slowly shuffled out carrying Jetta in her arms. Jetta looked happy and energetic.

Stepping out of my truck, I said, "Good morning, Mrs. Jones! And good morning to you, Jetta."

"Good morning, Andrew. I will be praying for you and Jetta today. I hope her blood sugar isn't too far off."

I lifted Jetta from Mrs. Jones's arms and hugged the woman's frail neck. I felt a quick kiss on my cheek and a soft pat on my shoulder. Placing Jetta in the front passenger seat of my truck, I shut the door and walked around to the driver's side. Mrs. Jones was standing by her favorite elm tree watching hopefully.

When I arrived to work, I carried Jetta into the clinic and set her on the treatment table.

"Ok, Jetta, just a little prick on your ear. I need to check your glucose now."

I discovered through the years of practice

that talking to my patients often had a calming effect on their demeanors. And in this case, I sensed that Jetta could understand my intentions.

Lightly, I poked the inside of her ear with a tiny needle and placed the glucometer strip to the blood droplet, listening for the glucometer's beep and anxiously awaiting the reading. Seconds later the number 320 flashed on the screen. "Ok," I thought. "It's high, but I can work with that."

I carried Jetta to an elevated kennel by the treatment room and went to retrieve a can of soft, low fat dog food. Before I could place her food bowl inside the kennel, Jetta began pawing at the cage door and whining loudly.

I opened the door. "There you go, Jetta. Eat up," I said as I put the food in front of her.

She devoured the offered portion, so I drew up four units into the insulin syringe. I had decided to increase her dose by one unit. Pinching the skin above her shoulders, I inserted the tiny needle to inject her insulin. Jetta never knew I gave the shot as she excitedly licked the bottom of her food bowl. I set my alarm for two hours, planning to check Jetta's glucose every couple of hours until the end of the workday.

I laid a thick, soft blanket in her kennel and patted it with my hand. "I told Mrs. Jones I would keep you comfortable. I will be back to check on you in a little bit."

Jetta's soul-searching eyes peered back at me trustingly.

Off I went to begin my day examining pets, but I periodically poked my head into the room where Jetta sat just to look at her. Each time I made an appearance, she would stand and whine softly.

Before I knew it, my alarm sounded to signal the two-hour mark, so I retrieved Jetta from her kennel and carried her to the treatment table.

"I hate having to poke you so much, Jetta, but I have to do it to keep you healthy."

I poked her ear again for a drop of blood, and Jetta did not squirm at all.

221.

"Good," I said aloud to Jetta. "Four units may be your new dose. We will see."

I was aiming for Jetta's blood glucose to run between 150 and 250, so I knew I was on track now. I reset my alarm for two hours and took Jetta back to her kennel.

By the workday's end, I was content with Jetta's response to the slight dosage increase.

I finished calling my clients, gathered my belongings, and then picked Jetta up in one arm.

"You ready to go home, little girl?"

Jetta wagged her stump tail and vigorously licked my face.

On my way to Mrs. Jones's house, I could not help but laugh at Jetta who sat upright in the front passenger seat, attentive to the world whizzing by. When I turned onto East 12th Street, Jetta stood on all four feet, whined anxiously, and wagged her whole rear end. She knew where she was, and her whining became louder as I slowly turned right into the short driveway. The garage door opened, and before I could exit my truck, Mrs. Jones came slowly out to greet us.

"Oh hey, Andrew! Was Jetta a good girl for you?" She asked while hugging me tightly.

"Yes ma'am, she surely was, as always. My most obedient patient!" We laughed together as I walked to the passenger door to get Jetta out.

"Come see mommy, Miss Priss," Mrs. Jones said with arms outstretched.

I carefully handed Jetta to Mrs. Jones but was afraid to let go because of Jetta's excited wiggling.

"Why don't I take her inside for you, Mrs. Jones? She's so happy she might twist right out of your arms."

We walked into the house, where I promptly set Jetta on the kitchen floor. Mrs. Jones sat in a dining chair, and Jetta bounded into her lap, licking Mrs. Jones repeatedly in the face.

Peering up at me with delight, Mrs. Jones

asked, "You say Leigh will be able to join us for supper tonight?"

"Yes ma'am, she should be here soon," I said, glancing at my watch.

"Good, good! Ok, Jetta, mommy has to get back to cooking now."

Jetta jumped to the floor and danced happy circles at our feet before lying down at her spot on the linoleum floor between the stove and dining table.

With a pork tenderloin in the oven, Mrs. Jones seasoned asparagus to stir fry and began boiling water for macaroni and cheese.

"Tell me about Jetta, Andrew. How is her sugar doing now?"

"She has responded as well as I could have hoped for." I said, bending over and scratching Jetta behind her ears. "I increased her insulin from three units to four, and that tiny amount has made all the difference. Let's do four units twice daily now. Let me know if she ever drinks more and urinates more frequently because that may be our sign that we need to increase her insulin again, but I will always check her out thoroughly before we ever adjust her dosage."

Mrs. Jones turned to smile at me. "You just will not know how much I appreciate you."

"I'm happy to help, Mrs. Jones."

Outside, a muffled car door slammed shut.

"Sounds like Leigh is here!" I reported.

"Oh good. Supper is almost ready." Mrs. Jones walked to the door to greet Leigh.

"Hey, darling! Come on in and give me a hug!" She threw her arms around Leigh's neck. "Please, sit down Leigh. I know you must be exhausted."

"I can help, Mrs. Jones. What do I need to do?" Leigh asked, offering to assist in cooking.

"Nothing, dear. It's ready. Please sit."

Leigh reluctantly sat in a chair at the table.

After we fixed our plates and I blessed the food, Mrs. Jones asked, "How long have y'all been married?"

I answered, "Going on five years now. We got married in December of 2010."

Mrs. Jones stared past me toward the den, a faraway look in her eyes. "I remember the day so well. I was eighteen and a half... 1949... would you believe the wedding service was actually in Cecil's home? Brides today would laugh at the thought! Cecil was the love of my life. He was nine years older than I and so mature. So handsome. He was my hero. He served four years in World War II in the Navy on a destroyer ship. Took part in *nine* invasions. Can you believe that? *Nine!* He didn't like to talk about it. He always said he didn't know how he survived, or why he did and so many fine men didn't make it back home. Anyway, he put the war behind him and moved on with his life. He created the most wonderful life for the two of us. I'm truly blessed that he found me. We were married one month shy of 46 years."

I was fascinated that Mrs. Jones did not appear sad as she spoke, but rather a nostalgic radiance emanated from her as she relived her memories.

"When Cecil died, I told myself I never would marry again. But God had other plans for me. He knew what I needed. A year or so later, Leonard entered my life again. I had known him practically as long as I can remember. In fact, I will show you a picture over there of the two of us standing together as teenagers." She pointed to a cluster of framed pictures across the room on a table. "His wife had passed away about the time of Cecil's death, and we were both lonely. When he approached the topic of marriage, I told him he was crazy. I did. But then I realized we needed each other. God sent him to me. Leonard was a wonderful man. Not many women can say that they have had two outstanding husbands!" Mrs. Jones laughed loudly.

She cleared her throat and looked intently at the two of us. "Now don't misunderstand me.

Marriage is hard. You must be willing to always work at it. People nowadays are ready to throw in the towel at the first sign of trouble. The difficult times are what can make the relationship so strong, figuring out *together* how to get through it."

Mrs. Jones paused for a few seconds.

"Enough of my preaching. Let's get these dishes cleaned and play some Rummikub!" She exclaimed with joy.

Mrs. Jones took her position at the kitchen sink and sang softly. Leigh and I assisted until the kitchen table and counters were cleaned.

"All right, my sweet children. Time to play! Andrew, would you grab the game?" Mrs. Jones asked, sitting in her chair at the table.

"Yes ma'am, if Jetta will allow me to get it," I laughed.

I knelt to the floor, reaching blindly underneath the couch as Jetta danced around me and licked my face. I could hear Mrs. Jones cackle behind me. Getting back on my feet, I carried the game case to the table and set it before Mrs. Jones.

I smiled as I looked around the room, at Jetta, at Mrs. Jones, at my wife. Mrs. Jones had become like a grandmother to us. Perhaps she thought of us as her grandchildren. She had such power in her presence, contradictory to her weak physical state.

    I unlatched the clasps on the leather Rummikub case and grinned at Mrs. Jones. "Are you going to let me win tonight?"

CHAPTER 11: "DO Y'ALL LIKE TO TRAVEL?"

I guess I could see it happening, but I must have chosen to ignore the signs. I was too emotionally invested to see the situation clearly.

"Andrew, will you come by tomorrow to have a look at Jetta? Her eyes are really cloudy, and she seems to be losing more weight." Mrs. Jones's voice sounded concerned. "And you know she doesn't feel good when she acts like she's not hungry."

"Yes ma'am, I will be there around 7:30 tomorrow morning. Let me take her to work for the day and check her glucose. Don't feed her breakfast or give her insulin shot. You know the routine." I hung up the phone and began to worry about Jetta's condition.

The next morning, I parked by the elm tree and stepped out in the muggy heat of midsummer. The garage clanked its way up, but Mrs. Jones did not step out. I hurried inside and found Mrs. Jones sitting in her dining chair holding Jetta and softly petting her thick, curly fur. Jetta looked up at me from behind hazy, opaque eyes with a frailty that was not her trait. Her abdomen had begun to sag and seemed to pull the muscles and skin of her back downward, revealing a look of emaciation. I really felt pity for the little dog.

"Hey, Andrew. Thank you for coming by. You see, she just doesn't have any energy," Mrs. Jones said quietly, patting Jetta's head gently. Jetta sat calmly... too calmly. Normally, she would have been dancing circles around my feet, whining for me to bend over and pet her. The pitter patter of doggie feet would not be heard today on the linoleum floor.

"Ok, Mrs. Jones, I'm going to do all I know to do for her," I said with as much optimism as I could muster.

I scooped Jetta into my arms as Mrs. Jones hugged my neck.

"I will give you an update this evening. I may have to keep her overnight. Let's just see how her sugar looks. See you soon, Mrs. Jones."

After arriving at the clinic, I placed Jetta on the exam table where she immediately sat down. She seemed exhausted. I carefully pricked the inside of her ear and watched a small drop of blood form on her skin. Holding the glucometer strip to the blood, I held my breath. I knew her glucose was going to be elevated but was shocked to see the number 557 flash on the screen.

"Oh no," I thought. This was not good. Her body was not responding well now, a fear that I had harbored since her diagnosis. Diabetes can be a horrible disease. It is sneaky, deceptively leading one to imagine years of quality health under the guidance of insulin. For a while, the body might respond favorably, but the diabetes quietly chisels away in its stubborn war of attrition.

Offering Jetta some canned food, which she normally enjoyed, I watched sadly as she turned her head the other way. No appetite this morning. I drew up 5 units of insulin, injected it under her skin, and placed her into the kennel with plenty of water and extra blankets.

I departed the room with a growing helplessness. Maybe, just maybe, she would respond to an increased insulin dose.

Throughout the day, I crossed my fingers and checked her blood glucose, but the results were disappointingly unchanged. Her levels never dropped below 450. She looked miserable, so I called Mrs. Jones.

"Hey, Mrs. Jones, I'm sorry to say this, but Jetta hasn't responded well all day. Do you mind if I keep her a day or two longer and put her on IV fluids? I think that will perk her up a bit," I said hopefully.

"Andrew, I trust you to do anything you think you should do for her. You know that. I will be praying for y'all." Her voice sounded amazingly strong.

"I will certainly try," my voice trailed off. "I will call you tomorrow."

"Thank you, Andrew."

We hung up our phones, and I resumed my focus on Jetta's care. I shaved her arm, placed an IV catheter, and connected the fluid line.

"This ought to make you feel a little better, Jetta."

I peered into her hazy eyes and put my head on her muzzle. Her thirteen-year-old body just could not hold out much longer. But I had to try.

As the workday came to an end, I took extra time to ensure that Jetta was as comfortable as could be for the night. Though I did not want to leave her, I placed my hopes in the revitalizing effects of the IV fluids. I had managed to spoon feed her a small amount of baby food, satisfying my desire to get any food at all into her empty stomach.

The last one to depart the building, I flipped off the lights and said, "Goodnight, Jetta. Hang in there. We are all pulling for you."

My key rattled the door lock the following

morning while I anxiously entered the clinic. Immediately, I hurried to Jetta's kennel. Turning on the room light, I peeked inside and saw Jetta sleeping.

"Jetta, you ok?" I spoke quietly to her.

She sleepily lifted her head with squinting eyes. It was too soon for me to tell if she was any better at all. I opened the kennel door, picked her up, and softly pet her head.

"Let's see what your blood sugar is this morning, little girl," I said, carrying her to the exam table.

Holding my breath, I drew her blood and placed it in the glucometer.

"Please be lower. Please be lower," I begged to the small device.

259!

Ok, I could accept that reading. My increase to 6 units the evening before seemed to be working.

"Do you want some breakfast?" I asked her wishfully.

I grabbed a jar of baby food, opened the top, and scooped out a small portion to offer. Jetta cautiously licked the spoon and then swallowed the offered amount.

"Good girl!" I patted her on the head. "See if you can eat some more."

As I fed, her appetite seemed to increase. My hopes grew.

"What do you say we call your momma? I bet she is waiting by the phone for an update this morning." I grabbed the phone from my pocket and dialed Mrs. Jones. It only rang once.

"Good morning, Mrs. Jones!" I said with an air of positivity.

"Good morning, Andrew. And how is my little Priss Tail doing?"

"Well, her sugar came down a good bit overnight, and she ate better this morning too."

"Does this mean she can come home today?" Mrs. Jones asked hopefully.

"Possibly so. I'm going to see how the day goes, and then I will let you know for sure."

"Good. Good. I will have something for supper that I can whip up really fast if you do come today. Bye bye, Andrew."

By 6:00 PM, I was feeling the emotional strain of Jetta's case, a numbing fatigue settling on me. I was not completely happy with the results of the day, but Jetta's blood glucose proved to be significantly more stable than the day before, although not quite within my target range. I decided to maintain Jetta on 6 units for several days to allow her body time to adjust to the increased dose, then I planned to recheck her at the beginning of the following week.

Calling Mrs. Jones, I reported the good news that Jetta would be going home. I set Jetta in the front seat of my truck, and she seemed to become more energetic, knowing that she was going home.

The shadows had covered the yard when I turned into the driveway. Predictably, the garage door opened for me, and out limped Mrs. Jones into the late afternoon heat.

"I'm so happy to see the two of you!" Mrs. Jones cried out to Jetta and me. "The house is just too quiet without you, Jetta."

Hurriedly, I went around the truck to retrieve Jetta from the passenger seat. A spark shone in Jetta's eyes, and her short tail began to wag furiously. The little dog was home.

"Come see me, my sweet Jetta!" Mrs. Jones laughed as Jetta licked her in the face.

I continued to hold Jetta since I was afraid that Mrs. Jones might unintentionally drop her.

Mrs. Jones ushered me inside and then asked, "Will Leigh be joining us tonight?"

Nodding my head, I responded, "Yes ma'am. She will be here shortly."

"Oh wonderful! I was hoping she would be able to come."

Setting Jetta on the kitchen floor, I watched

proudly as she danced her usual happy circles around our feet. She seemed to feel well again. I smiled at the sound of the pitter patter of doggie feet.

"I do believe you gave her a new lease on life," Mrs. Jones said while pointing a thin finger at the little dog. "I just pray she continues to feel ok. I'm worried that these last few weeks have really taken a toll on her body."

I could see the deterioration all too well... not only in Jetta, but in Mrs. Jones also.

Changing the subject of conversation, I asked, "What do you have planned for supper tonight, Mrs. Jones? The oven sure smells delicious."

"Poppyseed chicken casserole. I remember Leigh saying that it was one of her favorites," she said beaming.

I inhaled the aromas and closed my eyes. I loved this place.

Once Leigh arrived, we fixed our dinner plates, blessed the food, and began to eat. Jetta lay sleepily at Mrs. Jones's feet underneath the table.

"Do y'all like to travel?" Mrs. Jones asked suddenly with an interested look.

Simultaneously nodding our heads, we answered, "Yes." I then added, "We stay too busy to do much traveling now though."

Mrs. Jones raised her eyebrows in a sterner look and said, "If you enjoy traveling, then you should make time to do it. It's important. Life is about experiences, and you can learn so much from going places." Her firm tone softened. "I used to love traveling, seeing new things, meeting new people... One of my favorite trips was out to Vancouver with the church group. We went out there nearly twenty years ago. May and June of '97 I believe it was. If you have never seen those gardens in full bloom, then buddy, you are in for a treat. A flower lover like me can't get enough of the sights and smells." Her eyes looked dreamily across the room. "One spot was so beautiful with the sun shining brightly on all the flowers that I got our group together on some steps nearby and led them in singing "How Great Thou Art." I wanted to give God the glory for everything beautiful in our lives." She leaned back in her chair and smiled. "I do hope y'all get to go out there one day. I know you would enjoy it, as I did."

She closed her eyes and inhaled slowly. "The last trip I ever took was out to California. I had a great time, but I do believe the beaches of Florida are prettier. I think we take Florida for granted since it is in Georgia's back yard." Opening her eyes, she continued, "I have always loved the beach. It is a reminder of how magnificent God is.

I cannot look out over the ocean and not think about God's immense love for us."

She nodded at us approvingly, looked at the empty dinner plates, and with a quick grin said, "Who's ready for a game of Rummikub?"

CHAPTER 12: "AND I ALWAYS WILL"

It had been six weeks since Jetta's last overnight hospital stay. During her subsequent rechecks, her glucose had been erratic, and I had a growing concern that I was losing control of her challenging diabetic condition. I resisted the negative thoughts, but deep down I knew the reality.

Stepping out of my house in the cool, damp air of pre-dawn, I looked up at a hazy half-moon overhead. The eastern sky revealed no hint of the coming light.

My headlights illuminated the two-tone bark of Mrs. Jones's favorite elm tree as I turned into the driveway. Up went the garage door beckoning me forward; normally it was inviting, but not this morning. Hesitantly, I walked in, past the Chevy Impala and through the breezeway door. Up the few brick stairs, I paused to take a deep breath then turned the doorknob leading inside the kitchen. Mrs. Jones had already unlocked the door but did not greet me.

Instead, she sat in her dining chair holding

Jetta in her lap, kissing the little dog on top of the head over and over. Her tear-streaked face said it all.

Mrs. Jones turned her reddened eyes toward me and tried to speak, but no words came out.

Leaning over to hug her frail neck, I muttered, "I'm so sorry, Mrs. Jones…"

After a few seconds, she whispered, "I just don't want…" Her voice cracked, and she began to cry with her head lowered onto Jetta. "I just don't want my sweet Jetta to suffer. It's not fair to keep her here any longer. I think it's time…"

I marveled at this lady. So strong in her faith. So grounded. Able to see clearly through the foggy clouds of emotions. As a veterinarian, it is often my duty to advise an owner when euthanasia might be the best option. Some pet owners refuse to arrive at the conclusion on their own. But not Mrs. Jones.

"Yes ma'am," I responded sadly, my hand softly petting Jetta's back. I swallowed hard. "Do you want to be with her when I do it?"

Without looking up, Mrs. Jones quickly replied, "No, I will tell her goodbye right here. I want you to take her. I don't want anything back, not even her collar. Please take her bed, too. And her crate. I just can't stand seeing it all without her. I don't need anything to remember her by because she will be right here," she held her hand to her chest.

Ignoring the time, I patiently waited while Mrs. Jones said her final goodbyes to the last canine friend she would ever know.

Finally, lifting Jetta to me, Mrs. Jones kissed her one last time on the muzzle and whispered, "I love you, Jetta, and I always will."

I bit my lip, trying to retain some semblance of composure.

Quietly exiting the house cradling Jetta in my arms, I focused on what I had to do. This was my job. I placed Jetta in the front seat of my truck one last time. She had no strength to sit up. Her body was gone.

When I arrived at work, I administered a sedative to be sure Jetta was thoroughly relaxed and then sat down with her. As her body went limp, I thanked the little dog for bringing Mrs. Jones into my life.

I then grabbed my syringe filled with the pink euthanasia solution, wiped my eyes, and slowly administered the thick liquid into her arm's vein.

There was a peace in the room as she drifted away, and I sat with her for some time, gently petting her lifeless body.

As the well-known veterinarian, James

Herriot, once said, "If having a soul means being able to feel love and loyalty and gratitude, then animals are better off than a lot of humans."

I expect to see Jetta again.

CHAPTER 13: "WOULD HAVE BEEN GOOD FRIENDS"

Of course, it was not the same. The "pitter patter of doggie feet" was not to be heard anymore. Mrs. Jones slowly opened the door, and Leigh and I walked inside to hug her. The initial sadness hung over us, and I noticed that there were no signs that a dog ever occupied the house. Mrs. Jones had removed all tangible items connected to Jetta... except one (that I would realize later).

Showing her true resilience, Mrs. Jones brought up the matter first. "I miss my little Jetta so much, but I'm going to remember her for who she was and the many good times we had. I'm going to be happy when I think of her. You know, she will be my last one. I am too old to get another dog."

Mrs. Jones did not want to block Jetta out of her memory. Rather, she wanted to relive and preserve the memories. The quote by Alfred Lord Tennyson flashed through my mind: "'Tis better to have loved and lost than never to have loved at all."

Suddenly, the mood lightened as we told "Jetta stories." Mrs. Jones's eyes sparkled, recalling

Jetta as a puppy.

"My previous dog, Beau, was getting older, so Leonard and I decided to get a puppy. We loved Beau so much that we wanted another poodle like him. This time we chose a black female. Sweet Jetta was born on July 12, 2003, and was the cutest little thing we ever did see. Black as the Ace of Spades. Jet black. That's why I named her Jetta. She was the smartest dog I've ever been around."

Mrs. Jones looked out her bay window at the darkening day and paused for several seconds.

"Jetta seemed to know things even before I did sometimes. Like the time when she became so restless, barking and spinning circles at her leash hanging by the door. I got the message that she wanted to go outside for a walk. She pulled me around the corner of the house and down the street. Two policemen were just arriving to a house on the little side street, and I asked what was going on. They informed me that someone had just stolen a car from that driveway. I was first on the scene. Now tell me how my Jetta knew that? That little Priss Tail felt like she had done her duty and proudly led me back home."

Mrs. Jones laughed, a look of amusement on her face.

We heated leftover food for supper and sat at our usual places at the dining table.

I was asked to bless the food and then came the expected question: "Did you have any interesting vet cases, Andrew?"

Yes, I certainly had quite an arsenal of fascinating animal stories, but I needed a special case, one to make Mrs. Jones feel good. I delved into my memory files in search.

"Have I ever told you the story of Ralph?"

I knew I had not...

...The puppy presented to the clinic because of frequent vomiting over the previous few weeks. My boss, Dr. B, had gone through the usual checklist of potential puppy problems. However, this tiny, six-week-old Boston terrier seemed healthy other than being half the size of its littermates. Still, something just was not right. Years of experience and expertise prompted Dr. B to perform a fairly infrequently used diagnostic step in the continued quest to discover the culprit of this puppy's symptoms. A barium study is when we syringe-feed barium, a thick, white liquid that shows bright white on radiographs (X-ray), down into a pet's mouth to be swallowed and carried through the entire digestive tract. This process can offer us a clearer view of an obstruction that might be lurking inside the animal. And so, Dr. B squeezed an acceptable amount of the messy liquid into the puppy's mouth where it was gulped into the esophagus. Immediately, one radiograph was taken;

one was all that was needed. No denying the answer to this medical riddle now. All could easily view the problem why this puppy could not hold down its food. There, just above the base of the heart, the esophagus ballooned to an unimaginable size, filled with the obvious white barium liquid. Something was physically preventing the barium's passage from entering the stomach, and veterinarians are trained to recognize this rare birth anomaly— persistent right aortic arch, a condition in which one of the blood vessels from the heart that should regress and disappear after birth does not go away. This extra vessel leads to an encircling of the esophagus like a restrictive band. As the weeks progress, food stays retained in the esophagus, which chronically stretches it into a type of storage sack. The dilated state of the esophagus damages its peristalsis muscles, therefore rendering the esophagus useless in its designed propulsion of ingesta into the stomach. Naturally, these puppies do not have much food squeeze past the obstruction, so they are underweight and regurgitate frequently. The strangulating vessel must be surgically ligated (tied) and cut in order for a puppy to survive, but this surgery is not for a general practitioner like Dr. B. After explaining the heartbreaking news to the puppy's owners, Dr. B advised referral surgery to a specialist, but the clients did not have sufficient funds to pay for the expensive surgery. The decision was reached that the puppy should be euthanized, so Dr. B grabbed the bottle of euthanasia solution, drew one cc into a syringe, and placed his hand on the puppy's tiny front leg in preparation for injecting. Looking into the puppy's eyes, Dr. B turned his head and set the euthanasia syringe on the table. He knew he had to try. Never before had Dr. B attempted this harrowing thoracic surgery, but he had nothing to lose. First, he informed the owners of his decision, and they happily agreed not only to the surgery, but also to relinquish the puppy to Dr. B as his own pet, should the procedure prove successful. Next, Dr. B studied the surgery textbook on his approach and landmarks. The hand of fate was steering the course. Confidently, Dr. B stepped into surgery, made his incision, and quickly found the target— the persistent right aortic arch. Nimbly tying the blood vessel and transecting through to relieve the restriction, his hands worked with precision. Time was of the essence, and soon the little puppy was in the recovery ward and breathing well. However, there is a lasting effect of the esophagus muscle damage from the prolonged stretching: permanent loss of peristalsis (or movement) in the esophagus. For food to reach the stomach now, gravity had to be used. A child's car seat equipped with safety straps became the meal chair for this puppy, whom Dr. B named Ralph. The enforced upright feeding position ensured the food's passage effectively into the stomach, and once inside the stomach, the ingesta carried on through the remainder of the digestion process normally. Ralph was soon to be the veterinary clinic mascot and was often seen cruising on the lawn mower or motorcycle with Dr. B. Ralph was truly an exceptional dog with a human-like spirit, much like Jetta...

"And that's the story of Ralph, thanks to Dr. B who couldn't give up on the little puppy."

I looked up at Mrs. Jones. She had a distant, peaceful look in her eyes as she stared across the room.

"What a heartwarming story, Andrew. I will have to meet Ralph one of these days. I bet Jetta and Ralph would have been good friends."

"I bet so, Mrs. Jones. I bet so," I replied, closing my eyes to imagine the two dogs playing together.

After supper, we cleaned the dishes like all times before, and without prompting, I walked to the couch, knelt down, and swept my hand underneath to grab the Rummikub case. Pausing briefly while on my knees, I pictured Jetta darting back and forth to lick my face. I could not help but laugh to myself.

As I set the game case on the dining table,

Mrs. Jones shuffled to the TV cabinet, pulled out a VHS tape, and fed it into the VCR.

"Have y'all ever seen Carol Burnett?" Mrs. Jones asked without turning around.

"No ma'am," I responded.

Mrs. Jones clapped her hands, turned around, and limped slowly back to the table.

The Carol Burnett Show is a comedy from the '60s and '70s. I had never even heard of the show before, but Mrs. Jones seemed to know every word. Her eyes sparkled as she laughed. Nothing it seemed would interfere with her joy and fun that night. While playing Rummikub, we watched and listened to the show well past ten o'clock. Not even old grandfather clock could mess with our visit.

Glancing down at the spot on the linoleum floor between the dining table and stove, I smiled because I knew. We all knew.

Jetta was, indeed, still with us.

Opening the red envelope two days later, I slid the card out to read. On the front was a watercolor bouquet of colorful flowers, and on the inside were the printed words in bold: **Thanks For Being There**. Underneath these words, Mrs. Jones had written, *And you were!* She underlined it three times. Nothing more was written. Just a simple statement from the heart of a woman with genuine gratitude.

CHAPTER 14: "I KNOW I NEVER TOLD Y'ALL THIS"

Yet the lives of all the noblest and strongest people prove... that the endurance of hardship is the making of the person. It is the factor that distinguishes between merely existing and living a vigorous life. Hardship builds character.

(L.B. Cowman and James Riemann, Streams in the Desert)

"Do you know what kind of plant this is?" Mrs. Jones asked as she stiffly bent her hunched body over to touch the long leaf blade.

"No ma'am, I sure don't. I've definitely seen it before though." I searched my memory to find its name but to no avail.

"Mother-in-law's tongue," she revealed, gesturing with a sweep of her hand.

"That's a funny name," I laughed. "It looks more like a snake."

"Well, you are right on, Andrew. The snake plant is another nickname!" She let out a quick laugh. "Many mothers-in-law do have tongues like snakes. Fortunately, yours, Andrew, is as sweet as they come. And what a cook she is! Those chicken and dumplings she made me were just fantastic."

She stared at the small pear tree that had already dropped its fruit for the year and commented in a reflective tone, "Family is so important... It's a blessing that we too often take for granted. It warms my heart that you and Leigh both love your parents so much."

We heard a car pull into the short driveway and turned around to see Leigh parking by my truck under the elm tree. Still in her hospital scrubs, Leigh ambled through the white gate that led into the backyard.

"Oh hey, Leigh, I am so happy you could join us! Come give me a hug."

Slowly, we walked the perimeter of her yard as Mrs. Jones talked of her various plants that she had nurtured through the years. Mrs. Jones had to cling to my arm to brace herself across the uneven ground. We came to several blueberry bushes that were planted along the east line of her fence, and I reached down to touch their leaves.

"Mrs. Jones, we have a few blueberry bushes, but they aren't doing too well. And every time the berries begin to ripen, the birds eat them all." I shook my head thinking of our poor production.

"You should try covering them. There are

nets to put over the bushes to prevent the birds from getting to them. That's what I do. I have to. Those darn squirrels can still find a way to get some of them though." She pointed above her head to the pine tops. Several squirrels were scurrying along the high branches, unconcerned of our intrusion in their yard.

"You see, the only pines around are on the property line," she said pointing toward the fence. "When Leonard and I first moved here, we had twenty-three pines cut down. I wanted my yard open to be able to plant what I wanted, and I also worried about those tall trees falling on the house if I didn't get rid of them."

Against the backside of the house was a beautifully colored flower bed, and upon closer inspection, I realized that numerous flowers were fake. Mrs. Jones had interspersed the faux flowers in such a way as to not be obvious. I laughed to myself. That was one way to help the surrounding plants look healthy. But then, the sad realization also hit me that Mrs. Jones could no longer get outside much like she loved to do and likely felt the need to enhance her yard's appearance with the fake flowers.

We followed Mrs. Jones into the breezeway leading to her house, but instead of going into the kitchen door, Mrs. Jones grabbed the doorknob to the glass sunroom on her left, a room that Leigh and I had never entered. The room was warm. The air was stale. There was a slight musty odor. I could tell that she had not opened that door for some time, and Mrs. Jones confirmed my assumption.

"I guess I don't come in here much like I used to. Oh, how times change..." She looked out at the shadowy lawn below. "This actually used to be a screened porch, but I finally got fed up with all the pollen every year, so I glassed it in." In almost a whisper she spoke, "I used to love this little room..." her voice trailed off.

I gazed around the small room at the wicker furniture. All pillows were neat and orderly.

"Sit down, sit down, y'all." Mrs. Jones took a seat in one of the single chairs while Leigh and I sat on the couch next to her.

Mrs. Jones took a deep breath, looked out the windows, and let out a long sigh. She seemed hesitant to speak.

"I know I never told y'all this, but I never could have children..."

I did not look at Leigh though I knew she was especially intrigued as I was. We had occasionally discussed the kids in the photographs throughout Mrs. Jones's house, uncertain as to whose children they were. And of course, we did not dare to ask. This topic of children was coming at a tough time for us as we had been through a long, unfruitful year of back-and-forth travel to a reproductive specialist in Jacksonville, Florida. The five and a half hour round trips starting at four in the morning had begun to take their toll on our emotions. Month after month we awaited the news of our earnestly prayed for gift of being able to have a child of our own, only to be disappointed. Still, we hoped.

Mrs. Jones continued, "Cecil and I chose to adopt... twice. Our first baby girl was so beautiful, so sweet. Reba Mae. We loved that girl. Never knew a thing was wrong for nearly a year and a half, but then she just quit acting right. Not eating well. Spitting up. Seemed like she was having trouble swallowing. We noticed she was losing weight. We took her to the doctor a few times, but he thought we were overreacting because we were adoptive parents who didn't know any better. Then that doctor realized that we *were* right. Reba had a problem with her esophagus. He attempted surgery to fix her condition, but it was too late. She died November 18, 1957."

Her lip quivered, and her voice cracked, but she continued.

"I was so mad at the doctor at first. Then I prayed to God to give me healing strength, and He took my hand and led me away from all my anger. I am sure that I will see that precious baby again in the Kingdom of God."

Smiling through her tears, she wiped her nose.

"Our second girl we adopted a year later was healthy in body..." Her sentence trailed off. She paused and looked down at the floor, then out the windows again. "Sometimes I wonder if we did something wrong. I guess it's natural to blame yourself. What could have been, you know? We never could really control that girl. We loved her and loved her. We treated her as our child. But something wasn't right with her... her mind. She was untamable. Our relationship was shaky. She finally ran away. Wanted nothing to do with us. I have asked God why. What did we do wrong? All I can do is trust in Him and His plan. There is a reason, I know. I just have to keep on having faith."

Following Mrs. Jones's stare out the window, I witnessed a few elm leaves fall to the ground. I thought of little Reba Mae. Then, I thought of the second child. Where was she now?

Mrs. Jones shifted her weight forward and rocked herself up on her feet. "Come on, my dears. This old woman needs a game of Rummikub...."

CHAPTER 15: "THE SECRET TO PARENTING"

"Blessed is the man who expects nothing, for he shall never be disappointed" (Alexander Pope).

This statement had become our mantra. Time and time again, Leigh and I received the discouraging answer to our question. A numbing mindset pervaded our hopes that we would ever have a child of our own.

Today was different.

"Hey, Mrs. Jones!" Leigh and I shouted in unison through the phone.

"Oh hey, you two! And how are my precious friends doing?"

"We are doing great. Actually, we are doing better than we could have imagined. Mrs. Jones… we are going to be parents!"

Mrs. Jones's elation was as genuine as if the baby had been her own. She certainly knew what we had been going through.

"Oh! I am so happy for y'all! You two are going to make the most wonderful parents. That is one blessed baby. I thank God Almighty for this amazing news."

"Thank you, Mrs. Jones. I sure hope we are half the parents you think we will be," I laughed.

"How about y'all come see me one night this week, so we can celebrate. I will cook for y'all, ok?"

"We would love to, but please let us bring something to add to the meal."

"No sir-ee! Y'all just bring yourselves. That's all. Just your smiling faces. Oh, you just don't know how happy this makes me. I love you two so much."

"We love you too, Mrs. Jones."

We arrived at the same time. I had worked later, and Leigh had left the hospital at her usual time of 7 o'clock. We parked and together walked past the favorite elm tree, through the garage, and into the small breezeway with the three brick steps. The kitchen door lock rattled for a few seconds, and the door squeaked open.

"Do come in, and give me a hug, y'all!" Mrs. Jones commanded while trying to stretch her weak arms upward.

We had noticed over the past few months that her back seemed more arched, her neck more stiff, and her face thinner. She had a difficult time reaching to give me a hug. To walk about her house, she had to grasp objects— tables, counters, chairs, walls, anything to aid in keeping her balance. Basic functions were becoming difficult.

"Sit down. Please sit. I am almost finished cooking. Y'all have worked all day and need to rest," Mrs. Jones said selflessly, always concerned of our health over her own.

I looked at the stove with green beans and black-eyed peas. In the oven cooked baked chicken and diced red potatoes.

Shaking my head in wonder, I said, "No ma'am, we will help you."

She smiled. "Ok, then, if you insist. Pull that pan of chicken out of the oven, if you would, please. It's actually quite heavy to these old, tired arms."

Slipping two large, silver serving spoons into the beans and peas, Mrs. Jones exclaimed, "This is such a special occasion tonight!"

She turned around, motioning with her hand for us to serve our plates.

"You know, parenting is a demanding commitment that many people do not take seriously. You will be raising the next generation in line. The future depends on how well your children are taught and disciplined."

Leigh and I began filling our plates with food as Mrs. Jones resumed: "I'm not sure why people nowadays say that spanking a child is harmful to their psychological development. Spanking has worked successfully for eons and eons. If you ask me, we are doing much more harm to these kids by NOT spanking." Mrs. Jones paused to laugh quietly and picked up her plate. "I guess people would say I'm old and outdated."

Once our plates had been served, I helped Mrs. Jones sit and scoot to the dining table. I walked around to my chair directly across from her, and Leigh sat to my left like always.

Mrs. Jones clasped her hands and smiled. "Andrew, will you please say the blessing?"

"Of course, I will."

I thanked God for our time with Mrs. Jones and for our unborn baby. Then I prayed something that I had not pre-planned. I asked God for the strength to guide our child in Christ's name. Before even opening my eyes, I heard Mrs. Jones speak.

"And that, my Darling, is the secret to parenting."

I opened my eyes to see Mrs. Jones smiling back at me, a radiance shining in her eyes.

"The greatest thing you can do as a parent..." she cleared her throat and raised her trembling, splotched hand, "is to lead your child to Christ. It's that simple. Don't over complicate the process of raising a young-en."

I took a sip of water and asked, "But how do we do that, Mrs. Jones?"

Her eyes locked on mine. "You have to

accept Christ yourself, of course. He's already in us all. We just have to let him into our hearts."

"And another thing," she continued. "Don't underestimate the power of song in a child's life. I hope you will sing to that baby as often as you can. Song has a way of opening up the soul, no matter your age."

Mrs. Jones looked left and stared for several seconds. I looked too and noticed that she was gazing at Leonard's black cowboy hat hanging on the wall.

"Leonard and Cecil both loved to hear me sing. Oh, how I wish my old voice could still perform, but this thyroid cancer has taken that away from me. That's ok though. I can hum pretty well," she said defiantly.

Mrs. Jones lifted a finger in the air. "One more piece of advice for you new parents. Read to that little one every day. Your words will imprint on his or her growing mind, and the intimate time with a child in a book will help strengthen your bond together."

Suddenly, Mrs. Jones began pushing away from the table, struggling to stand. I hopped up from my chair and hurried around the table to assist her.

"Thank you, dear. Pardon me, but I must use the restroom," she said as I lifted her to her feet.

I watched as she unsteadily shuffled toward the hallway, her hunched back casting a prominent shadow in the low light from the den.

After several minutes, Mrs. Jones returned, and said, "I didn't tell y'all, but I nearly got stuck in the bathroom last week. I simply didn't have the strength to push myself back up. I finally did by bracing one arm on the counter and the other hand on the toilet paper roll. What a place to get stuck, huh?" She laughed with good humor. "I got my yard man to come in the next day and install a rail on either side of the toilet to help me pull myself up. It works like a charm."

How could I not be amazed by this woman's incredible optimism?

We ate, and we talked. We laughed. We cleaned our dishes. And, of course, we played our Rummikub well into the night.

But I could not get the nagging thought out of my head that Mrs. Jones looked too feeble to be on her own.

CHAPTER 16: "SHE TOO WOULD FLY AGAIN."

The faithful elm tree greeted us as we pulled into the driveway. Its limbs were bare on this cold, rather depressing, winter day. Always the first to see us arrive, this symbolic tree reminded me of the hope that lay in each visit with Mrs. Jones.

Now, I viewed it differently, for this would be the last time I would park beneath it. In time, other cars would park here, but not mine. For the past five years, this elm could help tell my story with Mrs. Jones.

The sky was a mixture of sparse blue ladened with dense, white clouds. The breeze carried over us from the west and created the soothing whispers through the longleaf pine branches high above. The cosmos were gone; the winter's freeze had taken their bright colors.

I soaked it all in.

The still scene was disrupted by the unrhythmic clanking of the garage door rising to allow our entry. Mrs. Jones was watching out her window… like she always did.

Slowly, we walked inside the garage, past

the silver Chevy Impala in its dormancy and into the cold breezeway, right past the sign that still hung to the left of the door, the sign that reminded me of Jetta. This sign, I realized, was the only thing Mrs. Jones had kept related to Jetta.

Hesitantly, I grasped the kitchen doorknob, found it unlocked, and pushed it open to step inside with Leigh behind me.

Mrs. Jones was expectantly waiting, seated in her dining chair with her hands in her lap. Though her body weak, her eyes glowed with surprising strength. She was a fighter. She was an optimist. She was going to enjoy this visit, no matter what lay ahead of her.

"Oh hey, you two!" She exclaimed, attempting to throw her arms out wide. "Come give me a hug."

We hugged Mrs. Jones, and I felt her soft kiss on my cheek. She did not stand.

"How are you doing, Mrs. Jones?" I felt that I should ask this question as a simple courtesy, even though I knew her response.

"I'm hanging in there... Enough about me though. How are y'all? Tell me, Leigh, how are you feeling now? That precious baby boy should be getting close now."

Leigh set the Zaxby's food bag on the table. It was the first time Mrs. Jones had allowed us to bring supper.

Leigh and I understood why Mrs. Jones loved cooking for us. It was a way that she could feel a sense of purpose while her independence slowly vanished. And now, even that was taken from her.

As we sat around the table, Mrs. Jones asked, "Andrew, will you please say the blessing?"

I paused a few extra seconds before beginning to speak. I absorbed a fleeting view of Mrs. Jones, hands clasped in front of her, head bowed, and eyes closed tightly. I could see her faith. Everyone who ever knew her could see it.

"So, Andrew, any interesting vet cases today?" She smiled, opening her eyes after my blessing.

I thought for a moment. Yes, I had the perfect story for tonight. A symbolic one no doubt.

"Yes ma'am. We have actually been treating a bald eagle..."

...Shooting a bald eagle is a criminal offense. After all, it is our national bird, a symbol of freedom. Why anyone would try to kill one, I will not know. A week prior, the DNR officer in our area was called to investigate an injured bald eagle alongside one of the plentiful country dirt roads. A .22 bullet had pierced one side of its breast, disabling its ability to

fly. Though the immediate wound was not technically fatal, the eagle would surely die if left to fend for itself. My first glimpse of the bird brought a feeling of sadness as I looked at the once majestic raptor, which was now in pitiful shape. Severe dehydration and starvation had turned its frame into a sad remnant of its former self. Its head hung ominously to its chest, and the breathing was shallow and rapid. Jumping into action, Dr. B and I quickly syringe fed the listless patient and doctored the infected wound. A sense of pessimism pervaded the mood, but I knew there was a chance for recovery. We just needed to be patient. Day after day, the eagle improved and finally began to eat on its own. Arrangements were made to send the bird to a wildlife rehabilitation facility in Florida with the expectation of eventually releasing it back into the wild at a wildlife management area outside of Tifton. Sometimes all that is required for our animal patients is quality nursing care. This eagle would fly again...

Mrs. Jones was smiling. I saw her in a different form. No longer the frail elderly lady sitting hunched at the table. Mrs. Jones was like this eagle— beautiful, strong, resilient.

She, too, would fly again...

We ate, and we talked for a while like nothing would change, but then Mrs. Jones brought up the topic we wanted to avoid.

"Judy is going to come tomorrow and help me pack up my things."

Judy, the wife of a nephew, unselfishly devoted her time to Mrs. Jones, often driving to Tifton from Tallahassee on a moment's notice. I loved Judy for that.

Pointing to the formal dining room where we rarely entered, Mrs. Jones said, "Before y'all leave tonight I have something I want you two to have. But first, let's play some Rummikub!" There was joy in her eyes as she said those words.

I wondered if this would be our last game of Rummikub as I slowly walked to the couch. Bending over to reach underneath, I closed my eyes to feel Jetta's tongue on my nose again.

I opened my eyes and looked around. Though Jetta was not there, I felt her presence. I slowly rose to my feet and carried the basket to the table. Mrs. Jones grabbed the game case, unlatched the top, and poured the game tiles in a pile.

There was a persistent thought I had all the while we played our game. This night, I did not lose track of time. I wanted to, but I could not. It was as if the powers of the Rummikub game and dining table, for the first time, were suppressed.

As the minutes ticked by, I became increasingly aware of the unyielding grip of time on my life. Eventually, I realized our chatting had subsided, and the house was quiet.

Mrs. Jones finally broke the silence and said, "Come in here. I have something I want to give to you." She unsteadily stood and led us into the secluded formal dining room, which was cluttered with boxes. In the shadowy corner on the right by a side table, sat a large cardboard box.

Mrs. Jones pointed and said, "This is for y'all."

Kneeling down, I opened up the top and peered inside. I saw a complete china dinnerware set, white with a dark green border circling and a thin gold line on the very outer edge.

"I can think of no better couple to give these to," Mrs. Jones said with an enormous smile stretched across her face. I knew how much this gift meant to her. It was like a symbol of all the meals she had cooked for us through the years. It was a tangible gift to remember her by, and I know she felt peace in the thought.

My mouth tried to say thank you, but nothing came out. I was leaving for the last time, and I knew it. I stole a parting glance around the house. The Beanie Babies high on the shelf. Leonard's black cowboy hat on the wall. The stove where she cooked. The sink where she sang. Jetta's spot on the linoleum kitchen floor. The favorite elm by the driveway. The cosmos in the yard.

And the table... the table where we ate, where we talked, where we played all those games of Rummikub.

That table was where we had just played our last game of Rummikub.

Our last game of Rummikub.

CHAPTER 17: "ALL THOSE MEMORIES"

Knocking on the front door, baby carrier on my arm, I heard quick footsteps approach. The door swung open to reveal Butch and Judy welcoming us into their Tallahassee home.

The friendly, robust man said, "Y'all come on in. Aunt Frances is right this way."

Eagerly, we followed, uncertain of how Mrs. Jones would look. I rounded the hallway corner and held my breath. In one of the bedrooms, Mrs. Jones sat upright in a chair with a spry look and gleam in her eyes. I breathed an inward sigh of relief. She looked surprisingly well.

Arms stretched, she sang, "Come here, you two!"

Leigh and I took turns hugging her, and then Mrs. Jones focused on the baby carrier.

"And would you look at that precious baby boy! I do have to get my arms around him."

Unbuckling Grayson from his carrier, I gently laid him in Mrs. Jones's lap. My little boy instantly bonded with her and began vigorously sucking on her finger.

"This sweet baby has quite a bite!" She remarked as Grayson gummed away at her finger. "It does this old body good to hold a baby again."

Leigh and I watched as Mrs. Jones quietly rocked Grayson in her frail arms.

"Let's take a picture," I suggested.

"Are you sure you want this old hag in your photo?" Mrs. Jones joked. "I'm not looking my best!"

"You look beautiful, Mrs. Jones," Leigh said sincerely.

"Yes, you do," I added.

I took several pictures of Mrs. Jones and Grayson, and Judy took more of the four of us.

With a big smile, Mrs. Jones asked her usual questions. "So, tell me about y'all. How are you doing? Your parents? How's work going?"

This time, I chose not to ask about her health.

We sat and talked for a while before Mrs. Jones asked, "Any interesting vet cases lately, Andrew?"

Of course, I had one.

"Yes ma'am. I saw a young Akita dog that needed her kidney removed..."

...The older man looked concerned. I listened as he told me that his Akita, a large breed dog originally from the mountains of Japan, had not

been acting quite right since her spay surgery at another clinic several weeks before. "Baby used to be full of energy, but now she sleeps a lot. She started vomiting two days ago and won't eat at all," the man explained. As I started my exam, my hands made their way to the dog's abdomen where I felt what I thought was a very large mass. "Sir, I believe we need to do an X-ray on Baby to see what the abdomen looks like," I said in a worried tone. After taking the radiograph, I viewed the digital screen incredulously. The abnormal structure I had palpated looked like an enormous kidney! But what on earth would make the kidney that large? Only one way to find out... I informed the owner of the need for an exploratory surgery, and he readily agreed. Once inside the big dog's abdomen, I did not have to search to find the engorged kidney, as large as it was. I knew what the diagnosis was, even though I had never encountered it before: hydronephrosis. Something was occluding the urinary tract on that left side, causing a backup of urine to fill the kidney, rendering it like a water balloon. Then, I saw the root of the problem. Whoever had performed the spay several weeks prior had accidentally tied a suture knot around the left ureter (the draining tube from the kidney to the bladder) while ligating the left ovarian artery. The damaged kidney, I knew, had to be removed, and having done a nephrectomy once before in my career, I felt competent enough to do it again. Slowly, I teased off the stubborn connective tissue clinging to the kidney, and then very carefully, I tied the giant renal artery which fed the kidney. Removing the swollen organ, I admired it like a prize and felt a sense of pride that I had saved this big dog from a slow, agonizing death. Baby would be just fine....

We got lucky on that one." I smiled at the thought of the Akita riding happily on the golf cart again with her owner.

"Andrew, I do love those stories of yours. You have a gift," she said with a wink of her eye. "You care for people and their animals."

I studied Mrs. Jones sitting in her high-backed chair in the brightly lit room. Her eyes had a youthful flare unconcerned with her own health problems. She gazed past me and reminiscently said, "I sure do miss our Rummikub games. We had some fun, didn't we? Y'all were getting pretty good, too. Those nights when y'all would come over..." Her eyes looked distant, as she saw the past dance in front of her. "You will never know how much it means to me... that I have all those memories."

I thought of the many Rummikub games we had played, all the hours we had sat talking at that dining table. I wondered if I would ever play the game again. Where was her game case? I opened my mouth to ask, but Mrs. Jones began to speak again.

"I thank Jetta all the time for bringing the two of you into my life. My little Priss Tail was something else. Smartest dog I ever had. And she gave me such comfort living alone like I did."

Suddenly, Butch strolled through the doorway, unintentionally interrupting the conversation. "Aunt Frances says you like to garden," he said, pointing a finger at me.

"Yes sir. I sure do," I responded.

"Let me show you around my yard."

Butch led Leigh and me from the room where Mrs. Jones remained. We strolled around the three-acre lot, viewing and discussing the fruit trees and the recently vacant, rectangular garden plot. Butch said, "I sure have learned a lot about gardening from Aunt Frances."

I smiled at the thought, realizing how much I had learned from her. "Me too, Butch. Me too."

The day was hot, so we made our way back inside and into Mrs. Jones's room. We visited for a long time before we had to leave, but our departure was not sad. Mrs. Jones always had a way of brightening the mood, even in gloomy situations.

As we drove away in the summer heat, baby Grayson sleeping soundly in the back seat, I remembered that I had forgotten to ask Mrs. Jones

something.
    Where was her Rummikub game now?

CHAPTER 18: "HOW MUCH Y'ALL HAVE CONTRIBUTED TO MY LIFE"

The last day of March 2021, and three days past my birthday, Leigh and I took the two-hour drive to Tallahassee to visit with Mrs. Jones. She had been moved the previous year into a nursing home because Judy and Butch could no longer take care of her numerous physical ailments. Mrs. Jones's mind, however, was as sharp as ever, and she was not planning to give up easily.

COVID-19 had put a halt to our visits, but today we had called and made a special request to see Mrs. Jones. Of course, we had to wear masks and be checked for fever at the entrance to the building. A nurse escorted us to Mrs. Jones's room where we found her sitting in her high-backed chair by a single window overlooking the parking lot. Her head hung down, curved cruelly by her spinal disease, but her smile overpowered any physical pain that she possessed. Her smile did that every time.

"Hey, my sweet friends!" she said hoarsely, waving us over to her where she slowly reached up to hug our necks. I noticed that she could no longer stand. Her knees were more swollen than I had ever seen them.

"So, do tell me how y'all have been. Tell me about your two precious boys, Grayson and Everett."

We began to fill her in on our busy lives as we tried to balance parenting with our full-time jobs. As Leigh talked, I slowly gazed around the small room. On the wall beside her bed hung the oval picture of her and Leonard, which used to hang by Leonard's black cowboy hat in her kitchen. The hat was nowhere to be seen. Where was the hat now, I wondered.

On the other side of her bed was a framed picture of her first husband, Cecil.

Across from the bed stood a short bookcase. Two of the books I recognized immediately. Pointing to them, I said, "Mrs. Jones, those books you mailed us by David Jeremiah are excellent."

"Didn't you just love them?" she responded with a strong smile. "David Jeremiah is one of my favorite Christian writers."

Since the beginning of our friendship, Mrs. Jones had frequently mentored Leigh and me in our faiths in Christ and in how to live a life following the Bible. The paradox of Mrs. Jones's weak and failing body juxtaposed to her iron-strong spiritual being made me shake my head in awe. I saw a fierce soldier for Christ underneath her frail skin.

"Andrew, do you have any interesting vet cases to tell me about? You know I love them."

Thinking for a moment, I responded, "Yes ma'am. I had a dog last week with a nasty concussion..."

...The dog owner called me in a state of hysteria. "My boxer Boss just ran into a trailer hitch head on, and he's not moving at all! Oh my gosh! He was chasing the tennis ball and hit the trailer hitch full speed. There is blood everywhere! I think he lost his eye!" Attempting to calm the client, I cut in, "Ok, ok, just look and tell me if he is breathing." There was a short pause followed by, "Yes, he is breathing, but he's not moving... he's not moving... he's not moving..." Again, I felt the need to cut her off. I instructed the woman to get help to load Boss into the car so that she could bring him in as fast as possible. When they arrived at the clinic, Boss the boxer was sitting up in the car seat, but blood covered his face. I was waiting in the parking lot to carry the patient in. Trying to disguise my look of horror, I quickly hoisted the big dog and toted him to the operating room. His left eye was completely covered in blood making it difficult for me to tell if his eye was even in the socket anymore. A huge wound was apparent

directly above the left eye socket. Once anesthesia was administered, I started my triage exam, and to my surprise, I discovered that Boss's eye was untouched; the blood had poured down out of the wound above and congealed in a way to make the sight seem like the eye was destroyed. The trailer hitch, fortunately, had pierced the sinus cavity right above the eye, which acted as a buffer to lessen the blow to the brain. A concussion and a fractured sinus cavity were the only issues for this lucky dog. I pulled the pieces of shattered bone back into place and sutured the skin over the top. In time, the bone would heal with only a slight indention noticeable. Boss was back chasing tennis balls within a few weeks....

"What an amazing case!" Mrs. Jones clapped her hands, looking youthful for a moment. "I do think I missed my calling to be a veterinarian," she laughed. "Life will pass you by if you are not careful." She paused and looked out the window at the empty parking lot lined with stout live oaks. "I sure do miss our times together. Our dinners. Our talks. Our Rummikub. You will never know how much y'all have contributed to my life."

I had to interrupt her to say, "Mrs. Jones, I don't think you realize all that you have done for us."

She simply shook her head and peered out the window at the breezy spring day.

I began to ask where her Rummikub game was, but for some reason, I did not. Something about the question was awkward for me, as if implying that Mrs. Jones would not be alive much longer.

I shook the thought from my mind.

CHAPTER 19: "I WANT YOU TWO TO HAVE IT."

The day was intensely hot but typical for a South Georgia August 28th day. Leigh and I made the trip to Tallahassee, and we knew that this visit would be different. Judy had called me three days before to tell me that Mrs. Jones had taken a turn for the worse. Despite multiple doctors' opinions, she had outlived her life expectancy by several years.

I parked beneath a large, moss-cloaked live oak outside the nursing home. Through the car window, I could see Mrs. Jones's room. I wondered if she was sitting in her high-backed chair watching for our arrival.

As we entered the building, a pleasant nurse greeted us and said, "Mrs. Jones has been so excited to see y'all today. She has been telling me all about y'all." She paused and seemed hesitant to speak. "Mrs. Jones has unfortunately been in a lot of pain these past few days, so we have had to keep her on some pretty strong pain medication. Don't be surprised if she dozes off while y'all are with her today."

Following the nurse down the long hallway,

we came to a door on the right. Colorful flowers decorated the door sign with Mrs. Jones's name on it. "Appropriate," I thought. The nurse softly knocked a few times and slowly opened the door. Mrs. Jones was propped up in her bed with a sleepy look on her face. But then, her eyes became bright when she recognized us.

In a squeaky voice barely above a whisper, she said, "Oh, Andrew and Leigh. Thank you for coming to see me today. It does this old woman good just to see your smiling faces. Your phone calls are so enjoyable, but there is simply no substitute for y'all being here with me." She coughed hoarsely, and the nurse gave her a sip of water.

We hugged Mrs. Jones gently and took a seat on the love bench near the foot of the bed.

"Do fill me in on everything going on with y'all," she said. "How are your two precious boys doing? How about your parents? I keep all of y'all in my daily prayers."

We told her about family life, and though her eyelids looked heavy, she remained attentive to the conversation.

"And I must ask, Andrew. Have you had any interesting vet cases lately? You know that I love hearing about them."

It did not take me long to think of one

that was fitting for the occasion. "Yes, ma'am. Of course, I do," I laughed. "I had a little beagle with inflammatory bowel disease, but the real reason it was a memorable case was because of my conversation with the owner…"

…The elderly man stood up as I entered the room. Extending his quivering hand to shake mine, he thanked me for accurately diagnosing his beagle after multiple visits to different veterinary clinics. "I never knew that dogs could get IBD like people, but it sure gave Buppy a rough time," the man said, taking his seat again. "My wife loved this dog. I wish she could be here now. Not a day goes by that I don't miss her." I nodded my head, unsure what to say. Then, the man continued, "I tell you what, I look forward to the day that I can see her again, but one thing bothers me about the Bible's description of heaven. I don't care much about walking on streets of gold."

I gave him time to finish his thought, but after a few seconds, I said, "I believe that the streets of gold are a metaphor. I think those streets are going to be something that is beautiful to you…"

The man smiled wistfully as he said, "I want it to be a meadow, with flowers of every color, colors so vibrant that we cannot imagine." He looked at the ceiling and continued, "And my sweet wife holding my hand. Buppy trotting along at our feet, chasing butterflies, and jumping up and down.

I caught on to what the man was wishing for. "Well, sir, I believe heaven will be that for you and so much more. Instead of the streets of gold, you may be walking on the most beautiful flower-filled meadow with everyone you love."

The old man smiled, his eyes watering. "Thank you, young man. You don't know how much you helped me just now. After all the diagnostics, the surgery, the intestine biopsy, the confirmation of IBD, and the life-changing treatment that you gave to Buppy, this conversation today is the cherry on top. I will never forget you, Dr. Curtis. I believe that I will see you in that gorgeous meadow one day"...

"Oh, Andrew. The Holy Spirit gave you the words that you needed to speak to comfort that man. You are a man of faith, and you live your life showing it." Mrs. Jones smiled sleepily.

"Thank you, Mrs. Jones," was all I could say. I never felt as good about myself as Mrs. Jones did about me.

The three of us looked out the window, the day hot and bright. I thought of how close Mrs. Jones was to walking in that pretty meadow of flowers.

"Do tell me," she began, "are your two elm trees growing well? I often imagine your trees when I think of my favorite elm tree back in Tifton. Sometimes, I think of those two trees growing up just like your two sweet boys. Little did I know when I gave them to you that you would wind up having two children. I know your boys will sit under those trees, in time. And part of me will always be there." Her voice trailed off. Her eyes closed.

Slowly.

Slowly.

Looking at Leigh, I shrugged and wiped a tear in the corner of my eye. Whispering, Leigh and I talked about the day, about Mrs. Jones, about how weak she looked. We talked to pass the time, waiting patiently while Mrs. Jones slept fitfully. Her body twitched occasionally, and her lips moved as if she were speaking. After about fifteen minutes, Mrs. Jones lifted her head from her chest and struggled to open her exhausted eyes.

Realizing what had happened, she apologized: "I'm so sorry, Andrew and Leigh. How rude of me to doze off while y'all are here to visit."

We assured her that she need not apologize, and she suddenly sat up straighter in her bed.

"Andrew, before I forget, go over there and look under that chair by the window."

Obediently, I stood up and walked to the chair. Kneeling, I peered under the chair.

"The Rummikub case!" I nearly screamed.

Before I could say anything else, Mrs. Jones

spoke, "I want you two to have it, as a reminder of this old lady... I know that you will teach Grayson and Everett how to play, and my hope is that it stays in your family and brings y'all peace like it did to me through the years."

Leigh and I were having a difficult time speaking as we fought our emotions.

"I sure do miss our times together, but at least I have the memories, and I am taking those with me. I love you two children more than you know."

When we stood to leave, Leigh and I had to wipe the tears streaming down our faces. Hugging Mrs. Jones one last time, I whispered, "I love you, Mrs. Jones. Thank you for everything...." We all knew this was going to be the last time.

As I reached the door, I heard in a barely audible voice, "Keep sowing the seeds of Christ, my children. Keep sowing the seeds."

Those were the final words that I heard Mrs. Jones speak.

CHAPTER 20: "MAY THIS GAME BE A BLESSING"

The day felt different, literally. It had been several months since I had felt the air so cool. It was September 2, 2021, surprisingly early in South Georgia to have a taste of fall, and we had just endured an intense heat wave to finish the month of August. I was driving to work in Valdosta, admiring the blue sky on a cloudless morning, when my phone rang.

Glancing at my phone screen, I saw Judy's name on the caller ID. Sadly, her call came as no surprise. Five days earlier, we had left Mrs. Jones's nursing home, knowing that her time on earth was extremely limited.

"Hey, Judy," I answered in a low tone.

"Hello, Andrew. I'm sorry to call you so early, but I had to let you know that Aunt Frances passed away a few hours ago." Judy cleared her throat. "Honestly, it's a relief. She was in so much pain..." Her voice cracked and cut the sentence short.

"Yes ma'am. I know she was hurting. She was one tough woman and never complained."

"No, I don't believe I can recall a time

hearing her complain about anything," Judy responded. "And one thing that I am certain of right now… Aunt Frances is in heaven with Jesus. Her faith never wavered. She was one of the most solid Christians I have ever been blessed to know."

I smiled. "Yes, ma'am. I agree with that."

"And, Andrew?"

"Yes, ma'am."

"Mrs. Jones thought the world of you and Leigh. She used to tell me how much y'all did for her. She viewed y'all as her children. And that Rummikub game was something special to her. She was adamant that y'all should have it. She told me that it was so much more than a game."

The tears were trickling down my cheeks, but I laughed a response. "Yes, it is definitely more than a game to us."

"Have you opened up the game case since she gave it to you?" she asked.

"Yes, ma'am. I surely did. And I found the note." My mind drifted to a few days before…

…I slowly dragged my fingers across the brown leather game case with the green and red design. I ran my hand through the leather handle and then to one of the metal buckles. I flipped it up to unlock it. Moving my hand to the second latch, I repeated the unlocking motion. Pausing for several seconds, I closed my eyes, preparing myself for a potential flood

of memories. Memories with Mrs. Jones, with Leigh, sitting at the old dining table, talking and laughing into the night, with Jetta lying happily on the floor, the room still smelling of supper, the warm little home at 604 E. 12th Street with the elm tree by the driveway next to the orange cosmos flowers.

Opening the case, I peeked inside, not realizing that there might be something special to find. There, amidst the green, red, black, and blue numbered game tiles lay a folded piece of notebook paper. That certainly had never been there all the times we played, but now I found myself gently grasping the paper and beginning to unfold it. I recognized Mrs. Jones's handwriting instantly, that shaky yet legible penmanship.

"Dear Leigh and Andrew,

Y'all are so precious to me. You will never know how much y'all have contributed to my life. Our journey together on this earth has been blessed, and I do expect to see you two again. You are already on the right track, but you must continue to be soldiers for The King, our Father in heaven. Carry with you the Sword of the Spirit, and you will never lose a spiritual battle. It's a hard road but a happy road. Remember that. Wherever you go, you must keep sowing the seeds of Christ, and your harvest will be bountiful! If at all you feel discouraged, read my favorite Bible verse—Ephesians 6:11. It WILL give you strength, as it has for me through the years.

I love you two with all my heart (and I know we will see each other again in the love of Christ),

Frances Jones

P.S. May this game be a blessing to your family as it has been for me."

Wiping my eyes, I neatly folded the letter again and placed it back in the leather case. I knew that I had not played my last game of Rummikub....

CHAPTER 21: "HER NAME WAS MRS. JONES"

Out my bathroom window to the west, I see a reminder, a reminder of a life that was lived. It was a life that intertwined with mine. It was the life of a woman who gave me what she could give. She gave me wisdom, which I did not even know that I sought. She gave me encouragement, motivation, and happiness. She gave me nourishment for my seeds of Faith. And she gave me the two elm trees that I look upon now, such a good reminder. It was her favorite tree.

The elms grow each day. They grow with my boys as time extends further and further from when I was with Mrs. Jones. I see the trees every day, but some days they are different in a sense. On those days as the sun sets behind them with the last rays filtering through the dense canopy of leaves, I see the story that I lived with more clarity. I see the importance of friendships and the importance of knowledge and wisdom passed on. I see what Mrs. Jones means to me, to Leigh, to my boys. I can only hope to leave a legacy of such importance.

On the north woodline of my yard, I see

the bright orange cosmos standing proudly. Year after year, their seeds scatter into the pine woods to keep the cycle alive. Very little maintenance is required. It was her favorite flower.

On my bedroom dresser, I see the game case, the brown leather with the red and green pattern, the sturdy leather handle, the two metal latches. It was her favorite game.

And inside the case, the game tiles and a note, neatly folded. On the paper in shaky handwriting, an elderly woman's last piece of wisdom to a young couple.

Grabbing the case in two hands, I walk into my kitchen and set it down on the dining table.

My two boys peer at the leather and ask, "Is this the Rummikub game you have told us about?"

Indeed, it is, but there is a whole life story in that case that I have not told them.

Smiling, I look at my wife, at my two sons, at my dining table, at my house, at all my blessings. I realize that I have not played the last game of Rummikub.

And so, I begin, flipping up the metal latches and slowly raising the top. Looking at my two boys, I feel a smile stretch wider across my face. "Your mom and I had a friend once. Her name was Mrs. Jones…."

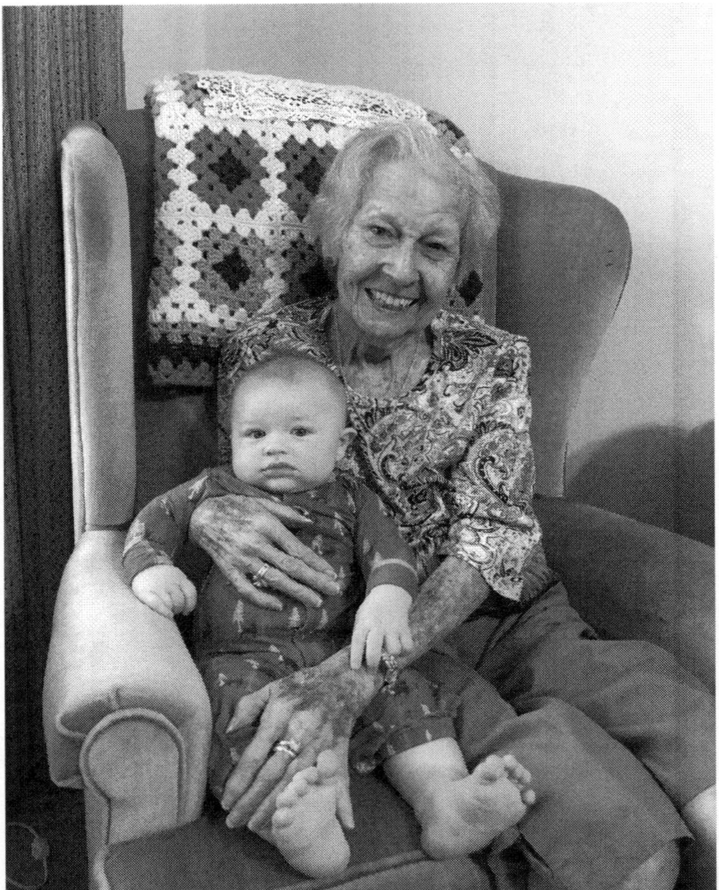

ACKNOWLEDGEMENTS:

As I have said numerous times, writing a book is a team effort, and I am proud of my team. My name is on the cover, but each letter of my name is held up by friends and supporters who believe in me as a writer, not just as a veterinarian. A veterinarian is what I am, but a writer is who I am.

Special thanks to my mom who is my number one fan and promoter, to my dad who has always shown his belief in me, to my wife Leigh who shares the same love as I have for Mrs. Jones, to my sister and rockstar publisher Sally Bartlett, to my talented editor Lydia Rogers, to my faithful design specialist Ann Carter, and to my loyal writing advisor, illustrator, and fellow author Matthew White.

I thank God for the wonderful people He has put into my life to make me a better Christian man, and I pray that I glorify God through serving His Son and my Savior Jesus Christ.

ABOUT THE AUTHOR

Andrew Carter Curtis

Andrew Curtis was born in Albany, Georgia. His love for animals and nature led him to the field of veterinary medicine. Andrew received degrees in Animal Health and Doctor of Veterinary Medicine from the University of Georgia and practices small animal surgery in Tifton, GA. He lives on the banks of the Alapaha River with his wife and two young sons and enjoys fishing, hunting, reading, and writing. Andrew believes that Jesus Christ is Lord and Savior.

Author of "Famous Catfish Stew," "Oh, Young Dr. Curtis," "Call of Courage," and "Humby the Hummingbird."

andrewcartercurtis.com

Made in the USA
Middletown, DE
18 February 2025